Maniacs Motorcycle Club
Standard Operating Procedure (SOP) Book

Mother Chapter Maniacs MC

The Colonel

Preface

The purpose of this book is two-fold.

First, and foremost, it serves as a consolidated source of Standard Operating Procedures (SOP) for the Maniacs Motorcycle Club. ®™ Other motorcycle clubs should feel to use it as a template for their own organizations. Better yet, we welcome you to consider the benefits of transitioning to the Maniacs Motorcycle Club. It is an easy process. Furthermore, your club would still probably be able to retain its original "flavor." Simply read on to see if you are interested.

This invite goes out to all bikers. If you possess a motorcycle and share our vision of a biker's lifestyle, you should consider joining the Maniacs Motorcycle Club.

Second, we want to destroy the myth of one-percenter motorcycle clubs as criminal elements.

One-percenter bikers are not what Hollywood and popular fiction has created. It's not Sons of Anarchy or the Mayans MC – talk about over-the-top absurdity. It's not Gangland. It's not about rape, pillage, and organized crime. It's not the equivalent of a Jack Reacher type of biker – commonly portrayed in popular fiction books (and unfortunately in supposed auto-biographies). Equating the term "outlaw" with "criminal" is purely an oppressive government conception embraced by a sensationalized media. Reality does not justify this tag. Sure, there are criminals and felons in some one-percenter motorcycle clubs. But no more than (actually probably less than) those found in government agencies and other large community organizations.

The entire one-percenter culture is based on the concepts of freedom, loyalty, honor, respect and a love for riding motorcycles. By their nature, one-percenters tend to be rebellious due to their dislike for oppressive rules and other attacks on their coveted freedoms.

The one-percent biker has a passion for a free society where you are judged by your actions, not your appearance. The desire to be left alone and not be harassed. This includes the self-respect to be able to stand your ground and not allow anyone to abuse or disrespect your person. Maybe, mainstream society is more tolerant of abuse/disrespect from others; but no one cares more about the concepts of freedom and honor than a one-percent biker.

One-percenters protect the elderly, young and the weak from being abused. One-percenters will not physically harm you unless you are caught preying on one of the classes of people just mentioned. That does not mean it's OK to shoot your mouth off at a one-percenter. That's likely to earn you a smack upside your head.

One-percenter motorcycle clubs are no more criminals than other historical groups fighting government discrimination, policies of oppression, and attacks on their freedoms. Patriots were considered outlaws. Many civil rights groups in the past were considered outlaws. Many current civil rights groups are considered outlaws. Peacefully demonstrating environmentalists are considered outlaws. For crying out loud, ancient governments described Jesus as an outlaw.

We sincerely hope reading this book will enable you to see through the government propaganda and Hollywood sensationalism.

Club Description

The Maniacs Motorcycle Club (MC) are a world-wide brotherhood of bikers who join together –
with a common set of beliefs and core values – to promote our love of riding and our vision of the
biker lifestyle. The foundation of the Maniacs MC is built on riding motorcycles and embracing
individual freedom. We are patriotic and support our nation's military. We are proud of our ancestral
heritage. We strive to continually improve our mind, body and soul through personal self-
motivation. We support other club members in their efforts to achieve the same. We honor and
protect our club, and the communities we live in, through whatever means are necessary. All this,
while celebrating life and living it to the fullest. We ride hard and party hard. New members and new
chapters are always welcomed.

Background of the Maniacs MC

There are three common definitions to describe a Maniac:

1. Person characterized by an inordinate or ungovernable enthusiasm for something.
2. Person who behaves in a very wild way.
3. Person who is violent.

The Maniacs Motorcycle Club embrace all three definitions. We prefer to be recognized by definition #1 – a brotherhood who is extremely enthusiastic about riding motorcycles and maintaining our personal freedoms. On occasion, definition #2 might come to the forefront – usually as a result of a personal freedom being oppressed. When we see a wrong being done, or when confronted, definition #3 will usually raise its head.

The Maniacs MC attempts to recapture the historic spirit of the following motorcycle clubs:

- 1935 – the original Outlaws MC of Chicago
- 1945 – the original Pissed Off Bastards (P.O.B.O.B.) MC
- 1946 – the original Boozefighters MC
- 1947 – the original Market Street Commandos MC

All four of these groups exemplified our vision of the biker lifestyle. These motorcycle clubs loved to ride their motorcycles. They hated to be constrained by "rules" and embraced their personal freedoms. They believed in living life to its fullest and did not really care what others thought. They were all self-disciplined groups and only displayed lawless behavior when antagonized.

The July 4, 1947, Hollister riots and the Labor Day weekend, 1947, Riverside riots in California demonstrates what happens when you take these normally self-disciplined groups and overstep your authority and try to repress the group's freedom. Many groups would have cowered and accepted the overzealous repression attempted on those memorable days in 1947. But these motorcycle clubs were of a different bred. They were willing to fight for their lifestyle. If you infringe on a biker's lifestyle, you always run the risk of having their triune-part of your brain – the R-complex – unleashed. That's exactly what happened during those historic motorcycle events.

We embrace "Wino" Willie Forkner, the founder of the original Boozefighter MC. Wino Willie's free spirit and dislike of rules is alive today and resonates in the form of the Maniacs MC. Although you have departed, we know you are still riding hard and partying hard. Godspeed, "Wino" Willie!

The official logo of the Maniacs MC is a tribal lion head emerging from flames. The tribal lion head part symbolizes the Maniacs' strength and courage. The tribal lion also signifies the power, loyalty and the honor of being a Maniac. Tribal lions can be scary and dangerous animals if provoked. The same thing can be said of the Maniacs.

The flame part denotes being divinely chosen and having spiritual zeal. The flames also signify being difficult to control and a force that demands respect. The same thing can be said of the Maniacs.

All members are expected to wear the club's tribal lion with flames logo on the back of their club colors centered between the top and bottom rockets.

Vision Statement

The mission of the Maniacs MC is to foster a spirit of camaraderie among members who share a common vision of the biker lifestyle and a common love of riding motorcycles and embracing individual freedom to its fullest.

Motto

MFFM – Maniacs Forever and Forever Maniacs.

This motto reflects the brotherhood bond among club members and demonstrates the high level of camaraderie, loyalty, and unconditional support among the Maniacs. All members are expected to wear a MFFM patch on the front of their club colors.

Philosophy of the Maniacs MC

The philosophy of the Maniacs MC is simple – put on your full colors and ride.

The Maniac celebrates life and lives it to the fullest. The Maniac rides hard and parties hard.

The Maniac is proud of his ancestral heritage and will fight to defend it. The Maniac wears his club colors to stark standard.

The Maniac offers no excuses. The Maniac mans-up to their family responsibilities, their job responsibilities, and their spiritual responsibilities. Next comes the Maniacs MC. We believe you do the club no good if you are failing in your primary responsibilities. The Maniac takes care of business and tries to be the best they can be and consistently seeks to be better.

When you need to feel an uplift, remember the pure essence of being a Maniac is the simple act of putting on your club colors and riding your motorcycle. It will always be the best medicine for whatever ails you.

MFFM – Maniacs Forever and Forever Maniacs

Keystones of the Maniacs MC

The foundation of the Maniacs MC is built on the simple act of riding motorcycles and embracing individual freedoms. Your participation as a Maniac and these keystone ideas are the real essence of what makes the Maniacs MC.

The Maniacs MC does not exist in some designated bar or clubhouse. The Maniacs MC exists on the road – riding your bike, grouped with loyal brothers, and proudly displaying the colors and logo of the Maniacs MC.

Motorcycles

Obviously, one prerequisite for joining our club is to have possession of a motorcycle. We accept all types of motorcycles. We prefer American-made cruisers (Harley, Indian, and Victory); but we defer on this preference to respect the freedom of the individual rider in choosing their own ride. All Maniacs are equal in the eyes of the club regardless of their brand of motorcycle.

We highly encourage regular club rides. These can range from informal, spur-of-the-moment rides to formalized, advanced-notice rides. The main thing is getting some members together, put on your colors, and ride. Postings for advanced-notice rides can be made by simple word-of-mouth, text-messaging, e-mail, or Facebook groups (if your local chapter maintains one). If made far enough in advance, you can have your rides posted in ***Maniac Ramblings*** – the club's semi-annual periodical.

In keeping with the theme of individual freedom, spur-of-the-moment rides do not need ride rules. However, for large organized rides, a Road Captain should be designated. We recommend this title be rotated among your club members on a ride-by-ride basis. If the ride involves a significant number of riders, consideration should also be given into assigning Blockers. As with the Road Captains, the responsibility of Blockers should be rotated among your club members on a ride-by-ride basis.

We highly encourage local chapter (LC) participation in charity & benefit rides, too. Attempt to get some type of favorable publicity for the Maniacs when participating in these types of rides. Also, local chapters are free to organize their own charity & benefit rides if desired.

Wearing of club colors is mandated on all rides. One of the few "rules" of the Maniacs MC.

Finally, one is always encouraged to put on their Maniac MC colors and ride solo.

Freedom

It is our fundamental belief that freedom is the basic tenant of all biker lifestyle. The freedom gained from riding a motorcycle cannot be put into simple words, it must be experienced. A non-rider cannot comprehend this experience. If they were able, they would no longer be a non-rider. Instead, they would be riding. It is the Maniacs MC's intent to promote this vision of the biker lifestyle.

It is all about freedom. Freedom from the daily grind. Freedom to unleash the repressed triune-part of your brain – the R-complex segment – as circumstances dictate. Freedom from excessive rules and oppression. Freedom to be your true self and to be unconditionally accepted.

The mother charter of the Maniacs MC has a minimum of by-laws to reflect this philosophy on individual freedom. We allow individual chapters to add their own by-laws; but these should only be the result of the chapter's individual personality and the desires of its membership and never for control over its members. We believe our members should be given maximum freedom in order to achieve their highest potential within the club. We trust in our club members to always strive to do the right thing. If they err in judgment, they will be expected to man up and take responsibility for their actions. The main thing is our members should never feel oppressed by the club's organization.

Obviously, our vision of the biker lifestyle means Maniacs tend to dislike rules. Indeed, the spirit of "Wino" Willie Foulkner remains alive and well in the Maniacs MC. Yes, this makes us a true one-percenter motorcycle club. This does not imply we dislike the other clubs – the so-called ninety-nine percenter clubs. On the contrary, we consider them to be our lost brethren. After all, they do ride motorcycles. They are simply of a different ilk. They really want to be like us; but we understand most of these folks have always been subliminally oppressed most their life through rules galore, and they really have a difficult time adjusting to life without having a multitude of rules to obey. Others are lost-cause obsessive-compulsive fanatics who can't handle the lack of structure.

The Maniacs dislike of rules – and other attacks on our freedom – is what sets us apart us apart as a true one-percenter club. We certainly have more in common with other real one-percenter clubs (not the phony ones depicted by big government and Hollywood fantasy) than we do with ninety-nine percenter clubs.

By definition, the difference one-percenter clubs and ninety-nine percenter clubs has nothing to do with being an outlaw and criminality. The Maniacs MC is classified as a one-percenter club because we refuse to accept the farce of a motorcycle club needing to be granted legitimacy through the American Motorcycle Association (AMA). The AMA wants the members of its sanctioned clubs to also be dues-paying members of the AMA. Plus, the AMA expects each club to pay an additional club fee, on top the member's fees, hitting a double-whammy on the rider's wallet. Not to mention, most of these ninety-nine percenter clubs require their riders to pay club dues on top of it all. Talk about a racket, maybe the RICO Act should be brought against the AMA.

The Maniacs MC does not collect dues. Our membership is free. Our approach more accurately reflects the lifestyle of a true biker – it is all about personal freedoms. Some local chapters might collect a nominal fee to offset the costs of having a permanent clubhouse, etc.; but it is not the norm for most chapters of the Maniacs MC. We believe a member's hard-earned money is better spent on maintaining their own bikes and in the appearance of club colors than to fork it over to some third-party organization who has the added gall to impose rules for sanctioning the club.

No third-party organization is needed to make the Maniacs MC legitimate. In our opinion, a motorcycle club only becomes legitimate through the collective souls of its members. In that respect, the one-percenter clubs are the truly righteous ones.

We proudly wear the 1% patch on our colors. It is a required club patch. The 1% patch simply reflects we are not sanctioned by the AMA and we have a personal dislike for rules. Unfortunately, the general public has this misconception on what the 1% patch really means. Due to fictitious television shows and movies, fictitious books, and exaggerated non-fictional accounts – including several by knucklehead academicians – the general public tends to equate the 1% patch with criminality. Nothing could be further than the truth. Unbiased individuals who have taken the time, and really attempted to know real one-percent bikers, know the real truth on the matter.

Often the 1% patch is associated with being called an outlaw club. Although this profile is not as egregious as being called a criminal organization, it is far from being accurate. Maniacs respect reasonable law and order and most of the front-line individuals tasked with enforcing those standards. What we dislike and distain are the nit-picky rules that infringe on our individual freedoms. This tendency might make us a little more rebellious than the average person. So, calling those who wear the 1% patch as rebellious is far more accurate than calling us outlaws.

We belief in the freedom to bear arms.

We believe in the freedom to protect our club, and the communities we live in, through whatever means are necessary.

The Big Picture and current attacks on our freedom
The Maniacs MC's concern about freedom is not simply about individual freedom, being rebellious, and having a general distain for rules. It is more global. The federal governmental is one of the biggest culprits threatening everyone's individual freedom. Do not get us wrong. We are patriotic and we support our military 100%. The problem lies in representation and the size of the federal government.

Our federal government is a bloated whale that is truly out-of-touch with its constituency. It appears our representatives only have ears open for big money and sniveling whiners. The average hard-working person is simply not being heard. The federal government have lost touch with what unites us and instead focuses on things which tend to divide us.

All this accomplishes is further division. The federal government does not know what is best for its populace. It seems the more involved the federal government gets, the more our individual freedoms are attacked.

The federal government needs to learn to step away. Let us resolve our own differences. Give state and local governments a chance and the latitude to address these issues. We are all more adept than the federal government at accomplishing things. Our federal government is broken. As alluded to, the federal government is a bloated whale, that's totally out of control, and becoming toxic to the cohesiveness of our nation by consistently attacking our personal freedoms.

The problem does not lie with the Republican party. The problem does not lie with the Democratic party. The problem lies in representation and the size of the federal government.

What's really scary
Consider these two facts (1) no one seems to know exactly how many federal government agencies exist, and (2) these agencies make most of the laws rather than Congress.

I kid you not! No one seems to know how many government agencies exist. Go ahead and google it. I guess the range is somewhere between 61 and 443 different agencies. How can you effectively run an operation without knowing how many agencies are in it? Ever wonder how well your tax monies are spent?

Do you know in the 1950's the Department of Housing and Urban Development, Department of Transportation, Department of Energy, Department of Education, Department of Veterans Affairs, and Department of Homeland Security did not even exist?

Are things significantly better in these areas today? Many could argue they are worse because of these bloated bureaucracies. The federal government is simply out of control. As it increases in size, our individual freedom gets less and less. The danger is exacerbated by the fact government agencies are the ones making most of the laws rather than Congress.

How many employees in government agencies identify themselves as public servants? Probably a miniscule number which is unfortunate because their output [laws] affect our freedoms. Instead, you are more likely to hear things like "I work for the Department of Transportation."

This is a dangerous mindset which shows loyalty to the agency instead of the populace it is intended to serve. Consequences to our liberties and freedom often take second seat to the self-preserving interests of the federal agency. Hence, the agency is inclined to make more laws to legitimize themselves and to attempt to justify their bloated size.

Meanwhile, the average hard-working individual is taxed over 50% of their income (if you include federal, state, and local taxes) in order to pay for this bloated bureaucracy. In turn, government insults us further by churning out more laws that further restrict our freedom and liberties. Talk about a vicious cycle.

Government must stop taking an active role in too many activities. At the state and local levels there is some resemblance of control. At least they know how many agencies exist at their level of government. It is the federal government that needs reeling in.

You could easily cut most of the middle and upper management staff of these federal agencies without impacting on its services. In fact, it might actually improve services since most of this upper staff waste time with meetings where they end up burdening front-line staff – the ones who really accomplish something and who directly work with the public – with often senseless work changes. How else does middle and upper management in government justify their positions?

Unfortunately, when Congress attempts to cut agency size, the end result is middle and upper management cutting front-line staff. This results in a public outcry since services get directly affected. In turn, the agency gets funding restored and everything goes back to status quo. An on-going saga of federal agencies out-smarting our congressional representatives.

In order to correct this situation, Congress needs to micro-manage and directly go after agency middle and upper level management staff with a scalpel. Government agencies have proven they are unable to accomplish this action themselves. They have become too self-serving. Drastic action is needed to include the outright elimination of some entire Departments and all of its associated agencies. Remember, prior to 1965, we survived as a nation without needing six of our current Executive Departments!

The growing size of our federal government endangers all of us. Not so much from becoming bankrupt; but from oppressing us with a constant bombardment of new laws and regulations. We know their intention is usually good. But they must change into the "public servant" mindset. They must weigh the consequences of their actions and how it impacts on our freedoms and liberties.

Individual responsibility

The Maniacs MC's concern about freedom also includes individual responsibility. Being a Maniac means you will take responsibility for your actions. We man-up to our short comings. Maniacs do not offer excuses. We do not view ourselves as victims.

Maniacs strive to continually improve our mind, body and soul through personal self-motivation.

Inactivity is a bane to Maniacs. We try to incorporate physical training programs into our lifestyles. Easily accessible, high-caloric, nutrient-empty foods are a bane to Maniacs. We try to eat good, wholesome, nutritious foods.

Although our education levels might vary, all Maniacs respect the ability to learn more about themselves, others, and the world. We continually seek new knowledge and experiences.

Individuals are free to practice their own spiritual beliefs within the club without judgment. We encourage all Maniacs to expand their spiritual awareness.

Organization of the Maniacs MC

In keeping with our theme of freedom, the Maniacs MC does not endorse any specific formal organizational structure.

The Maniacs MC attempts to offer the most in terms of freedom to its members. The mother charter contains very few by-law requirements for its local chapters.

Local chapters are at liberty to tailor the by-laws of the mother charter in order to meet the unique needs and expectations of their local members. The Maniacs MC recognizes the club's belief and core value system will change and evolve among its local chapters as new members are added and new local chapters are added. Having the ability to tailor the mother charter ensures the "flavor" of each local chapter will be kept unique and truly reflect the values and beliefs of its members.

The freedom of individual local chapters to add their own by-laws should never be abused. Creation of new by-laws and formal organizational structure should only be the result of the chapter's individual personality and the desires of its membership and never for control over its members. We believe our members should be given maximum freedom in order to achieve their highest potential within the club. We trust in our club members to always strive to do the right thing. To demonstrate that trust, our members should be given the freedom to be inclusive in making club decisions and be willing to take responsibility for their actions. It is one of the basic tenants of what we believe a biker's lifestyle should be. The main thing is our members should never feel oppressed. The essence of our club is to simply don colors, ride our bikes, and be free to enjoy life.

We believe the spirits of the original 1935 Outlaws, the original 1945 Pissed Off Bastards, the original 1946 Boozefighters, and the original 1947 Market Street Commandos never intended motorcycle clubs to have formal organizational structure nor the host of by-laws and rules usually associated such structure.

That said, some local chapters might grow to such a size as to necessitate some type of formal organizational structure. Although as a one-percenter group, we might tend to embrace chaos – especially since our members tend to be of better caliber than the average man and are usually fully capable of handling chaotic situations – there can reach a point in size where formal structure is needed.

If used, formal organizational structure will usually result in the creation of an Executive Board consisting of a President, Vice-President, Secretary/Treasurer, Sergeant-at-Arms, and Road Captain. Refer to the Mother Charter for more details on formal organizational structure.

If the local chapter does not incorporate a formal organizational – which is the recommended action for smaller local agencies and in keeping with the intent of the mother charter – it still requires two members to be assigned as point-of-contact (POC) for dealing with chapter matters. In most situations, an informal organizational structure will naturally evolve. A current copy of the Maniacs SOP Book and Mother Charter should be available for all chapter members to access regardless of organization-type.

Objectives of the Maniacs MC

To promote our vision of the biker lifestyle by wearing our club colors and patches when we ride and to promote this vision through the collective actions of individual group members.

To allow maximum freedom to our members. In general, we distain rules. It infringes on our individual freedom. Our mother charter contains a minimum of bylaws to reflect this philosophy. We allow individual chapters to add their own bylaws; but these should only be the result of the chapter's individual personality and the desires of its membership and never for control over its members. We believe our members should be given maximum freedom in order to achieve their highest potential within the club. We trust our club members to always do the right thing. To demonstrate that trust, our members should be given the freedom to make club decisions and be willing to take responsibility for their actions. It is one of the basic tenants of what we believe a biker's lifestyle should be. True freedom is constantly under attack and joining the Maniacs MC is one way to exercise your freedom.

To improve the overall health and well-being of its membership by encouraging physical fitness programs, fostering continuing education opportunities, and cultivating spiritual awareness.

To offer a brotherhood ↔ family ↔ friendship bond with other Maniac members. We expect most members to put family, job, and God first in their list of priorities and rightfully so. The Maniacs MC and riding your bike is intended to be something you look forward to amidst the daily grind. That said, do not take your decision to join the Maniacs MC lightly. If you are not certain whether the Maniacs MC can be a natural extension of your lifestyle, you should move on to another club or something else of interest. Once you pledge allegiance to the Maniacs MC you become a member for life.

To offer each member unconditional support throughout the endeavors of life. Each member should feel they are an important part of the Maniacs MC because it's really is the truth of the matter. Each member should feel accepted and comfortable among other club members.

To offer each member a place within the Maniacs MC where they are valued. Although the mother charter does not mandate individual chapters have an organizational hierarchy, some of the larger chapters might want to implement some type of structure through its own chapter bylaws. Regardless of whether your local chapter has an organizational chart, all Maniacs are to be valued. The simple act of wearing your colors and riding with the club (or by yourself) is always a significant act of value. Riding with colors (aka "flying your colors") is always something special and meaningful. You will always be contributing to the club by regularly performing this simple act.

To offer each member the laurels associated with the club's image and reputation. Once accepted into the Maniacs MC, members can wear the official logo and patches of the Maniacs MC.

To celebrate life and live it to the fullest. Ride hard and party hard.

Beliefs and Core Values

We acknowledge the overlap between the club's vision, philosophy, and its core values and beliefs. What's important to recognize is not the similarities, but to be able to recognize the differences.

The club's vision and philosophy will never change. They are permanent fixtures that will always be associated with the Maniacs MC. In contrast, the club's beliefs and core values are only a snapshot in time. As times change, we expect the club's beliefs and core values to change and evolve. Indeed, if we believe in maximizing the individual freedom of our Maniac brothers, we must respect their own personal beliefs and core values. As new chapters of the Maniacs MC evolve and as new members join the ranks of Maniac brothers, undoubtedly, the club's beliefs and core value systems will change, too.

This should be embraced because the club is really about its members. The beliefs and core values of an urban Maniacs chapter will be different from a rural Maniacs chapter. That is to be expected, and it will further enhance the cohesiveness within each local Maniacs chapter by allowing for differences of opinion among the multitude of Maniac brothers.

The club's vision and philosophy will never change. It is the two things ensuring cohesiveness among the many different local Maniac chapters. So, if you have a difference of opinion with the club's vision or philosophy, walk away now because those things will never change. However, if you have a difference of opinion with the club's beliefs and core values, we are interested in hearing about those differences.

As mentioned, the club's beliefs and core values are only a snapshot in time, meaning this list can change year-to-year. Also, each local chapter can modify this list to better reflect the beliefs and core values of the Maniacs within their specific chapter. In fact, this is encouraged. Be at liberty to modify this list to best reflect the beliefs and values of your local chapter.

Maniacs MC Beliefs

We believe all Maniacs should be proud of their heritage. Remember our logo denotes we have been divinely chosen.

We believe family and brotherhood are important elements in the life of all Maniacs.

We believe in being supportive of all motorcycle clubs. Although our value system is more aligned with our fellow one-percenter brothers, we still treat ninety-nine percenters as our brothers, too. The real deal is most motorcycle clubs get along fine with each other. It is Hollywood, big government, and the media who exaggerate and sensationalize isolated incidents. These culprits love to antagonize infighting among motorcycle clubs. Unfortunately, some clubs – both one-percenters and ninety-nine percenters – have bought into this bogus dissention trap. In the eyes of a Maniac, if you ride a motorcycle you are treated as brother. Let's stop being dumb stooges and bury our hatchets. We all face enough prejudice without being prejudicial to each other.

We believe big government suppresses individual freedom through its excessive laws and rules. Also, many organizations suppress individual freedom through excessive rules and procedures. The American Motorcycle Association being a prime example.

We believe we are an open target for being a recipient of "false news" because we wear a 1% patch. Although, we have pledged to honor and protect the communities we live in, the facade about one-percent bikers – created by irresponsible media and academia -- continues.

As already mentioned, due to fictitious television shows and movies, fictitious books, and exaggerated non-fictional accounts – including several by knucklehead academicians – the general public tends to equate the one-percent biker as being a violent criminal. As real one-percent bikers, we know the real truth on the matter. This might piss off some folks; but a Maniac is made of intrinsically better stock than most folk (refer back to our #1 belief about heritage). This might sound elitist but it a basic feeling shared among all Maniacs. We might not have been born with silver spoons in our mouths, we might not have had the educational opportunities of most, and we might not have had the luck to get a secure and good-paying job; but we are still divinely chosen. We are blessed with characteristics that money cannot buy nor education can teach. We possess loyalty, honor, and discipline – rare commodities in today's world. We have sustained drives to continue to evolve and be the best.

Our approach is "we do not seek to be understood as to understand." It's all about being intrinsically better stock.

We believe in the right to bear arms.

Also, we believe it is healthy to use all three parts of our triune brains – especially the one involving the R-complex. In our opinion, constantly suppressing your primitive brain is unhealthy and leads to deviant behavior. We all have a streak of wildness within us. It is healthy to unleash it on occasion. There would be considerably less mental health problems in the world if more folks took the opportunity to occasionally unleash the animal within themselves.

Maniacs MC Core Values

Two categories – what we like and what we dislike.

What we like

- We like motorcycles. Dahh!
- We like freedom.
- We like to ride hard & party hard.
- We like things involving personal development and growth. We like motivated individuals and gung-ho individuals. We like folks who aggressively pursue good health. Individuals who want to take care of their body, mind, and spirit.
- We like individuals who man up to their short comings and make no excuses.
- We like women who wear short shorts.
- We like good fist-fights.

What we dislike

- We dislike anyone who physically harms an elder, a child, or a dog. If observed, definite retribution will be taken. The R-complex will become engaged.
- We dislike excessive rules. Possible rebellious action could occur.
- We dislike oppression. Likely rebellious action could occur.

- We dislike quitters. We dislike individuals who are prone to making excuses. We dislike whinners. All three of these categories are despicable. Pure flotsam as individuals. One simply hopes their genetic material is not passed on. If our planet gets too crowded these should be the first folks to go.
- We dislike pussies and posers. In contrast to the previous three despicable categories, these two categories might be tolerable depending on any outside attributes these individuals might possess. Also, to clarify – we like pussy, it's pussies we dislike. If you do not know the difference, you are certainly not Maniacs material. Also, no apologies for these comments. If any of it offends you, suck it up and move on, and don't let the door hit you in the ass.

Chapter Surveys

Each local chapter of the Maniacs are expected to survey its member's belief and core value system once every two years basis (more frequently if needed). The results of the survey should be internally shared with its members and discussions should attempted as to whether to incorporate anything of significance into the chapter's bylaws.

Maniacs MC Highlights

- Only two members are required to start a local chapter of the Maniacs MC.
- Maniacs wear their club colors according to strack standards. The club's logo – a tribal lion head emerging from flames – is 100% embroidered.
- The Maniacs MC does not collect dues.
- The Maniacs MC offers the most freedom to its members. The mother charter contains very few bylaw requirements for its local chapters to enforce.
- Local chapters are at liberty to tailor the bylaws of the mother charter in order to meet the unique needs and expectations of its local members. The Maniacs MC recognizes the beliefs and core values will change among its local chapters as new members are added and new local chapters are added. Having the ability to tailor the mother charter ensures the "flavor" of each local chapter remains unique and truly reflects the values and beliefs of its members.
- The Maniacs MC has its own periodical ***Maniac Ramblings***.
- The Maniacs MC does not put the club in front of your family, your job, or God.
- The Maniac MC believes it is the function of the club to serve its members – not for the members to serve the club.
- To become a member, you need to (1) possess a motorcycle, (2) procure and properly maintain your own set of club colors, (3) fill out a written application, and (4) get sworn-in by an active Maniac in good standing.
- The Maniacs MC does not require a probate period.
- Stripped down to its true essence, being a Maniac is as simple as putting on your club colors and riding your motorcycle.

How to become a Maniac

The process is relatively easy.

First Step

You fill out an application. The application consists of three sections (see next page).

In the first section, you fill in personal information. In second section, you personally attest to being able to meet Maniac standards. In the third section, you pledge allegiance to the vision and philosophy of the Maniacs MC including acceptance of the traditional beliefs and core values of your local chapter. The application must be signed and sent to the mother chapter.

Usually an application takes three to four weeks to process. If you are accepted, you will receive an acceptance letter welcoming you to the Maniacs MC. If you have not received anything by the end of four weeks, it is best to check and verify we received your original application. We do not send rejection letters.

Second Step

Once you receive your acceptance letter, you become authorized to procure the club's colors. The second step consists of getting a complete set of club colors. This consists of the Maniacs logo, a top and bottom rocker, and five patches. The placement of the club's colors must be exact. It is highly recommended you have a professional seamstress or tailor attach your club colors.

Third Step

Once you have your club's colors ready to wear, the last step involves getting officially sworn-in by an active Maniac in good standing. The swearing-in ceremony varies from local chapter-to-local chapter. It can range from elaborate affairs involving many Maniacs and drunkenness and debauchery to subtle affairs involving sharing a beer with a fellow Maniac. It all depends on the "flavor" of the local chapter.

That's it! No dues......no hazing......no probate period.

You are now a full-fledged Maniac Brother with full-club privileges. The only thing left is to put on your colors and ride to your hearts content.

How to leave the Maniacs MC

One does not leave the Maniacs MC. Recall our motto: Maniacs Forever, Forever Maniacs. This motto captures the degree of club loyalty expected out of all Maniac brothers.

Although becoming a Maniac is a relatively simple process, it is a serious decision that should not be taken lightly. You should thoroughly read all you can about the club, and/or get briefed from an active Maniac member before deciding to join. We suggest you talk it over with your immediate family, too. We expect you to place the needs of your family, your job, and God before the needs of the club. We feel that kind of value system is essential for you becoming the best you can be. With those ingredients in place, you become a better functioning Maniac and a better overall asset to the club.

The club should be an important part of your life. The club should be treated as an extension of your family – a place where you are unconditionally accepted, a place to escape the daily grind, a place where you can put on your colors and ride with brothers and experience freedom ten-fold.

The club is setup to meet your needs over a lifetime and we expect a lifetime commitment in return. If the club's vision and philosophy does not fit well with you, do not apply. If the local chapter's "flavor" does not fit well with you, simply seek out another chapter or consider starting your own local Maniac chapter if you are able to find other bikers of like interest.

Reading "one does not leave the Maniacs MC" and a "lifetime commitment is expected" might initially appear scary. Do not confuse these statements with the fiction you might have read about in one-percenter clubs. That is pure bull-shit. You do not die or get the shit kicked out of you if you attempt to leave. Maniacs have your back. Maniacs protect their brothers. You might have an occasional fistfight with another Maniac brother; but a brother will never physically harm another Maniac brother. The meaning of "one does not leave the Maniacs MC" and a "lifetime commitment is expected" is more a state of mind about loyalty – expected out of all Maniacs -- than something to be taken literally.

Maniacs do have an option to request a sabbatical from the club. Sabbaticals usually last from one year to multiple years. Sabbaticals can be used for various reasons. They can range from needing to be a caretaker for a family member, to taking a spiritual pilgrimage, to going back to school, to being temporarily incarcerated. If you are granted a sabbatical, you will be kept in the club's communication loop but are not expected to participate in club activities. Maniacs lose their voting privileges while in sabbatical status.

Maniacs Motorcycle Club
Membership Application

Full Name: ____   Date:______________

Last   First   M.I.

Address: ____

Street Address   Apartment/Unit #

____

City   State   ZIP Code

Phone: ____________________________   Email:_______________________________

Local Chapter's Name (if known): ____

Preferred Alias (if desired): ____

I have reviewed the background history of the Maniacs MC. I have reviewed the objectives, beliefs, and core values of the Maniacs MC.

I personally attest to being able to meet Maniac standards.

Signature: ____   Date:______________

I have reviewed the vision statement and philosophy of the Maniacs MC. I personally pledge allegiance to the vision and philosophy of the Maniacs MC.

Signature: ____   Date:______________

Colors of the Maniacs MC

Once you receive your acceptance letter, you become authorized to procure the club's colors.

The complete set of club colors consists of the Maniacs logo, a top and bottom rocker, and five patches. The placement of the club's colors must be exact. It is highly recommended you have a professional leather worker, seamstress or tailor attach your club colors. Ensure they have the proper equipment for the task. Often shoe repair shops have the right equipment – it is worthwhile to give them a look, too

Colors are "flown" on leather jackets or leather cut-off vests to allow visual identification of club membership and to show the state association of the local chapter.

Back Colors

The back colors of your leather shall consist of the Maniac's logo, a top and bottom rocker, and a MC cube patch. No others colors are authorized on the back of your leathers.

Logo

The official logo of the Maniacs MC is a tribal lion head emerging from flames. The tribal lion head symbolizes the Maniac's strength and courage. The tribal lion also signifies the power, loyalty and honor associated with being a Maniac. Tribal lions can be scary and dangerous animals if provoked. The same thing can be said about Maniacs.

The logo's flames denote being divinely chosen and having spiritual zeal. The flames also signify being difficult to control and a force that demands respect. The same thing can be said about being a Maniac.

The club's logo is fully embroidered and approximately 12" in circumference. The logo shall be horizontally-centered between the top and bottom of the leather. The logo shall be vertically-centered between the leather's vertical side-seams. The actual center-point where the horizontally-centered and vertically-centered lines meet should land on the space between the top of the middle-two teeth (right along the top lip edge).

Top Rocker

The top rocker shall contain the club's name.

The length of the top rocker can vary from 14.0" to 16.5" measured from outside corner to outside corner. Use your judgment on what fits best on your size leather.

The club's name shall be centered on the rocker and shall be capitalized. A Copperplate Gothic font shall be used with black letters and a black border on white twill fabric.

The rocker shall be shall be vertically-centered between the leather's shoulder-seams. The rocker should be horizontally-centered so the middle of the bottom edge is about 1.5" above the top-most edge of the flames on the centered tribal lion's head.

Bottom Rocker

The bottom rocker shall contain the name of the state your local chapter is located in.

The length of the bottom rocker can vary from 14.0" to 16.5" measured from outside corner to outside corner. Use your judgment on what fits best on your size leather. Whatever your final decision, the length of your top and bottom rockers shall be of equal distance.

The state's name shall be centered on the rocker and shall be capitalized. A Copperplate Gothic font shall be used with black letters and a black border on white twill fabric.

The bottom rocker shall be shall be vertically-aligned with the top rocker. The bottom rocker should be horizontally-centered so the middle of the top edge is about 2.0" above the bottom-most edge of the flames on the centered tribal lion's head.

MC cube patch

The MC cube patch contains the capital letters MC and identifies the club as a motorcycle club.

The dimensions of the MC cube patch can vary anywhere from 2" to 3" in size. The letters MC shall be centered within the patch and capitalized. A Copperplate Gothic font shall be used with black letters and a black border on white twill fabric.

The MC cube patch shall be worn on the right side of the back.

The MC cube patch shall be horizontally-centered so its horizontal centerline is centered between the bottom-most edge of the top rocker's end and the top-most edge of the bottom rocker's end.

The MC cube patch shall be vertically-aligned so the inner edge of the cube patch is aligned with inner-most edges of the top and bottom rockers. Actually, in most cases (it all depends on the size of the MC cube patch) this brings the inner edge of the cube patch too close to the logo's right-side flames. If that is the case, you shall horizontally move the cube patch 0.25" to 0.50" to the right.

Front Colors

The front colors of your leather shall consist of three patches on the left front-side and one patch on the right front-side. Local chapters have the option to authorize the wearing of additional patches and pins on the front-side of your leathers; but under no circumstances should back colors be varied.

The required front patches are an alias patch, a one-percenter patch, a local chapter ID patch, and a MFFM patch.

Alias patch

The alias patch is worn on the right front-side and contains the member's preferred name.

The dimensions of the alias patch can vary anywhere from 3.0" x 1.0" to from 4.0" x 1.0" in size. The letters shall be centered within the patch. Capitalization and font type are left to the discretion of the member. Whatever style is chosen, black letters and a black border on white twill fabric are still required.

The alias patch shall be horizontally-aligned so it is aligned with your nipple line (think of an imaginary horizontal-line drawn across your nipples).

The alias patch shall be vertically-aligned so it is centered between the shoulder seam and the middle line of the front leather.

Local Chapter ID patch

The local chapter ID patch is worn on the left front-side and contains the name of your local chapter.

The dimensions of the local chapter ID patch can vary anywhere from 3.0" x 1.0" to from 4.0" x 1.0" in size. The letters shall be centered within the patch and two lines should be used for the lettering.

The first line should only contain the name of the local chapter with the first letter of each word capitalized and the rest of the word in lower case. An acceptable alternative is to have the first letter of each word in a larger-size font and the rest of the word in smaller-size font.

The second line on the patch should only have the word "Chapter" on it. The first letter of the word "Chapter" shall be capitalized and the rest of the word in lower case. As with the first line, an acceptable alternative is to have the first letter in a larger-size font and the rest of the word in smaller-size font.

Both lines shall be centered on the patch. A Copperplate Gothic font shall be used with black letters and a black border on white twill fabric.

The local chapter ID patch shall be horizontally-aligned so it is aligned with your nipple line (think of an imaginary horizontal-line drawn across your nipples). To ensure perfect alignment, the local chapter ID patch must be aligned with the right-side alias patch.

The local chapter ID patch shall be vertically-aligned so it is centered between the shoulder seam and the middle line of the front leather.

One-Percenter patch

The one-percenter patch is worn on the left front-side and identifies the Maniacs as a one-percenter motorcycle club. It shall be the top-most patch worn on your left front-side.

The one-percenter patch is a triangle-shaped patch and can vary anywhere from 3.0" to 4.0" in height. The patch shall be embroidered and have a black fabric background. The letter and border colors are left to the discretion of the member. White letters with a red border is preferred. However, the following color combinations are acceptable: white letters with a white border; yellow letters with a yellow border; orange letters with an orange border; and red letters with a red border. Whatever color combination is chosen, a black fabric background is still required.

The one-percenter patch shall be horizontally-aligned so its bottom-most point is about touching the top-edge of your local chapter ID patch.

The one-percenter patch vertically-centered on the mid-point of your local chapter ID patch.

MFFM patch

The MFFM patch is worn on the left front-side and is the Maniac's motto. It shall be the bottom-most patch – of the three mandatory ones – that are worn on your left front-side. The phrase "MFFM" is an acronym for "Maniacs Forever, Forever Maniacs."

The dimensions of the MFFM patch can vary anywhere from 3.0" x 1.0" to from 4.0" x 1.0" in size. The letters MFFM shall be centered within the patch and capitalized. A Copperplate Gothic font shall be used with black letters and a black border on white twill fabric.

The MFFM patch shall be horizontally-aligned so its top edge is about 0.25" below the bottom-most edge of your local chapter ID patch.

The MFFM patch shall be vertically-aligned with your local chapter ID patch.

Miscellaneous Patches and Pins

As mentioned, depending on local chapter "flavor," you might have the option to wear additional patches and pins on the front-side of your leathers; but under no circumstances should back colors be varied. Inquire with your local chapter to see if they have any type of earned-- patch system in place.

Wearing Colors

Colors are to be attached to leather not denim. Wearing of club colors is mandated on all rides. One of the few "rules" of the Maniacs MC.

You are also encouraged to where your colors whenever riding solo.

Maintaining Club Colors – Keeping Strack

One of your main responsibilities as a Maniac to maintain your colors to strack standard. First impressions are extremely important. It is often how others judge you. The Maniacs MC really does not care how you dress or groom yourself. But we certainly do care how you wear your club colors.

Recall it is not the intent of the Maniacs MC to collect dues. The club believes a Maniac's hard-earned money is better spent on maintaining one's motorcycle and in keeping club colors up to strack standards.

What does "keeping strack" mean?

Strack means you have your shit together. In regards to club colors, it is an adjective that defines an individual who keeps their colors far above normal standards. There should be no loose threads visible. There should be no stains on the logo, rockers, or any of the patches. There should be no frayed patches. All the required patches are exactly arranged the way they should be. Denim is taboo. Leather is the only way to go.

Concerns

Since you are required to buy your own club colors, they are yours to keep. The club logo costs between $40-45. The top and bottom rockers cost between $20-25 each. The five mandated patches (MC cube, alias patch, local chapter ID patch, one-percenter patch, and MFFM patch) cost about $5 each. Expect the total cost to run you somewhere between $105-$120 per set. We also encourage you to seek the services of a professional leather worker, seamstress or tailor in getting your colors attached to your leathers. Ensure they have the proper equipment to sew emblems on leather jackets/vests. Also, be sure to check out cobblers and shoe repair shops. The placement of the club's colors must be exact.

It is recommended you figure out the proper placement of your patches at home using a tape measure and ruler. Then outline your patch placements with tailor-chalk prior to getting them professionally handled. This makes it easier for the third-party sewing them. You might need to refresh the chalk lines when you drop off your stuff.

The cost of this service varies but expect to lay out between $40-$75.

Some folks express concern about wearing a 1% patch thinking it implies we are a criminal gang or it will antagonize another local one-percenter club. Total bullshit, brought on by reading too many fictitious books, and watching too many fictitious movies and TV shows. Forget about Gangland, the Sons of Anarchy and the Mayans MC. That's Hollywood embellishment.

As mentioned in the previous sections, there will always be narrow-minded folks who equate the 1% patch with criminality and nihilism. Simply ignore these ignorant folks. Their pea-brains cannot comprehend us. They fear us because of their own innate cowardice. Remember, we are better – we do not seek to be understood but rather we seek to understand. You have to feel sorry for ignorant and biased folks who probably go on living their lives in the same sad manner.

In regards to antagonizing other local one-percenter clubs, simply ponder the thought a little deeper. If anything, wearing the 1% patch will have a bonding affect. The Maniac's MC has more in common with other 1% patched clubs than clubs not wearing the patch. You will find other true one-percenters willing to warmly welcome you into the ranks of the 1% MC family. Sure, some knuckleheads might attempt to initially test you; but usually it is simply a bluff to weed out pussies and posers. One-percenters respect others who are willing to fight. If you show your willingness to rumble, they will back off and acknowledge you for the real deal and as a 1% brother.

Again, one simply has to stow away the ignorant misconception that one-percent bikers are criminals and nihilistic. Know your motorcycle history, we evolved from the same spirit as other one-percenter clubs. We all evolved from the same 1935 original Outlaws MC of Chicago; the 1945 the original Pissed Off Bastards (P.O.B.O.B.) MC; the 1946 original Boozefighters MC, and the 1947 original Market Street Commandos MC.

All one-percenter clubs love to ride their motorcycles. All one-percenter clubs hate to be constrained by "rules" and embrace personal freedoms. All one-percenter clubs believe in living life to its fullest and do not really care what others think. All one-percenter clubs are self-disciplined groups that only displayed lawless behavior when antagonized. All one-percenter clubs are self-disciplined groups that only displayed violent behavior when directly threatened. That is the REAL DEAL, Jack.

With so much in common, only an idiot would think wearing a 1% patch would antagonize other local one-percenter clubs. If anything, expected to be invited to more of their parties and activities. But again, certain elements in our society seem to enjoy trying to pit brother against brother.

Most of these small-minded individuals are not known for having high intellect (although they tend to be usually well-educated – many with PhDs or working on their PhDs albeit in some easy "soft" field of science like sociology or criminal justice).

Some folks also express concern that wearing a bottom rocker can lead to violent conflict with other one-percenter clubs. They use the 2015 Waco shootout as evidence stating this event was caused by a club wearing a "Texas" bottom rocker. What total bull crap!

Again, the same folks who express concerns about wearing 1% patches are the same ones expressing concern about bottom rockers. Simply engage your brain and give this some real thought. Why would two organizations, with much in common, resort to violent conflict over a patch that simply shows from which state the MC hails from?

The bottom rocker does not claim territory. It simply shows what state the MC hails from. Common sense should dictate the absurdity of such a claim. The real deal, Jack, is one-percenters are not always fighting with other one-percenters. On the contrary, one-percenters share common bonds, rarely have conflicts with one another, and often party together. But that does not sell newspapers, or books, or movies, does it?

There was a conflict between two one-percenter clubs resulting in the 2015 Waco shootout, but it was not caused by a club wearing a "Texas" bottom rocker. What most likely happened was the whole incident was incited by a small number of club members who were using too much juice (steroids), or more likely caused by a small number of meth heads (crank). If you have members who are juice heads or meth heads, you have loose cannons in your club – especially the meth heads. Help these brothers get treatment. If not, the next incident might be with a different bike club, or it might be with an innocent third-party member of your community, or worse-case scenario, it might be with your local law and enforcement. You can't have loose cannons in your clubs.

Colors for Associate Members

If desired, the spouse or significant other of a full member can become an Associate Member. Associate members may participate in club activities and events. Associate members may also wear club colors.

There is one important caveat for associate members who choose to wear the club colors – associate members are prohibited from wearing an alias patch. In place of the alias patch, the associate member must wear an associate member ID patch.

Associate Member ID patch

The associate member ID patch must be worn on the right front-side and contain the words "Associate Member." The dimensions of the associate member ID patch can vary anywhere from 3.0" x 1.0" to from 4.0" x 1.0" in size. The letters shall be centered within the patch. The first letter of each word should be capitalized and the rest of the word in lower case. An acceptable alternative is to have the first letter of each word in a larger-size font and the rest of the word in smaller-size font. Whatever style is chosen, black letters and a black border on white twill fabric are still required.

The associate member ID patch shall be horizontally-aligned so it is aligned with your nipple line (think of an imaginary horizontal-line drawn across your nipples). The associate member ID patch shall be vertically-aligned so it is centered between the shoulder seam and the middle line of the front leather. If the associate member decides to procure and wear club colors, they are expected to maintain them to the club's strack standard.

What sets the Maniacs MC apart from other motorcycle clubs?

Only two members are required to start a local chapter of the Maniacs Motorcycle Club.

Maniacs wear their club colors according to high standards. The club's logo – a tribal lion head emerging from flames – is 100% embroidered. The flames denote Maniacs as being divinely chosen and having spiritual zeal. The flames also signify being difficult to control and being a force that demands respect. The tribal lion head symbolizes the Maniacs' strength and courage. The tribal lion also signifies the power, loyalty and honor of being a Maniac. Tribal lions can be scary and dangerous animals if provoked. The same thing can be said of the Maniacs.

The Maniacs MC does not collect dues. The club believes a Maniac's hard-earned money is better spent on maintaining one's motorcycle and in keeping their club colors up to high standards.

The Maniacs MC offers the most freedom to its members. The mother charter contains very few bylaw requirements for its local chapters. Our biker lifestyle philosophy is all about freedom. That means the fewer the rules the better.

Local chapters are at liberty to tailor the bylaws of the mother charter in order to meet the unique needs and expectations of its local members. The vision and philosophy of the Maniacs MC emerged from the old-school (1935-1947) biker clubs. The vision and philosophy of the Maniacs MC will never change. It is the substance that bonds our local chapters together as one brotherhood. However, our beliefs and core values will change. They will change and evolve as new members are added and new local chapters are added. Each local chapter should have its own unique set of beliefs and core values that reflect the individual Maniacs within its chapter. Having the ability to tailor them into the mother charter ensures the "flavor" of each local chapter is always unique and truly reflects the actual values and beliefs of its members.

The Maniacs MC does not require a probate period. We would never expect anyone of Maniac-caliber to allow themselves to be subservient. All members are equal in the Maniac brotherhood. To become a member, you need to (1) possess a motorcycle, (2) procure and properly maintain your own set of club colors, (3) fill out a written application, and (4) get sworn-in by an active Maniac in good standing. That sounds simple, but it should not be taken lightly. You should thoroughly read all you can about the club, and/or get briefed from an active Maniac member before deciding to join.

Your local chapter can assist you in obtaining your own set of club colors. The club is setup to meet your needs over a lifetime and we expect a lifetime commitment in return. If the club's vision and philosophy does not fit with you, do not apply. If the local chapter's "flavor" does not fit with you, simply seek out another chapter or consider starting your own local chapter if you can find other bikers of like interest. If your confidence needs a boost, and you are not sure you can fulfill Maniac MC expectations, I suggest you speak with an active Maniac member before moving on. Starting baselines differ from new Maniac to new Maniac, but we all seek to improve and that's what's really important. Plus, you will have other Maniacs supporting your endeavors. You may not come into the Maniacs as being a badass but you will develop into a badass with the Maniacs.

The Maniacs MC requires the wearing of the 1% patch, but it does not put the club in front of your family, your job, or your spiritual needs. We are realistic and are not swayed by all of the fictitious television shows and movies, fictitious books, and exaggerated non-fictional accounts – including several by knucklehead academicians – which portray one-percent bikers as always being "over-the-top." The Maniacs MC, and riding your bike, is intended to be something you look forward to amidst the daily grind. You do the club no good by not keeping your priorities straight and keeping your shit together.

 The Maniacs MC maintains its own periodical ***Maniac Ramblings***.

The Maniac MC believes it is the function of the club to serve its members – not for the members to serve the club. Yes, the club is greater than the sum of its members in terms of its power and strength. But the club without members ceases to exist – end of statement. On the other hands, members always exist.

How to become a Local Chapter

The process is relatively easy. Two individuals are needed to start a Local Chapter. If one or both individuals are not full-fledged Maniacs, then the individual(s) must also submit a membership application. Both processes can be done concurrently.

There are no application fees associated with starting a new chapter.

First Step

You fill out an application. The application consists of three sections and an attachment. In the first section, you fill in local chapter information. In second section, you certify the candidate chapter will strive to maintain the traditions, beliefs, and core values of the Maniacs MC. In the third section, you declare the candidate chapter will pledge allegiance to the vision and philosophy of the Maniacs MC.

The required attachment is a membership roster. If any individuals are not full-fledged Maniacs, then those individual(s) must also submit a membership application. Again, both processes can be done concurrently.

The application must be signed by both point-of-contacts and sent to the mother chapter.

Usually an application takes three to four weeks to process. If the new local chapter is accepted, an official Certificate of Acceptance will be issued granting the local chapter full privileges within the Maniacs Motorcycle Club.

Second Step

Once you receive your Certificate of Acceptance, your chapter becomes official – a recognized and valued part of the Maniacs Motorcycle Club. The second step consists of ensuring all chapter members procure an appropriate local chapter ID patch.

The local chapter ID patch is worn on the left front-side and contains the name of your Maniac's local chapter. Refer to the section on "Colors" for more details on the local chapter ID patch.

Maintaining a Local Chapter of the Maniacs MC

The Local Chapter's responsibilities:

- Organize chapter rides and activities.
- Approve new members.
- Conduct swearing in ceremonies for new members.
- Ensure all members have access to the Maniac SOP Book.
- Tailor the Maniac SOP book with the chapter's own addendums.
- Ensure all members have access to Manic Ramblings.
- Create self-improvement opportunities for its members.
- If desired by the members, develop and implement an earned-patch system.
- Approve membership sabbaticals.
- Decide on a preferred means of communication for the chapter. Ensure chapter members are capable of communicating with one another.
- Designate two members to be the main point of contact with the Mother Chapter.

- Each chapter will be responsible for maintaining an updated roster of members including their contact information. This is normally the responsibility of the two members designated as being the main point of contact with the Mother Chapter.
- Each Local Chapter should survey its member's belief and core value systems on a once every two- year basis (more frequently if needed). The results of the survey should be shared with all chapter members and discussion should attempted as to whether to incorporate anything of significance into the chapter's bylaws.
- The belief and core value survey results – and an updated membership roster with contact information – shall be forwarded to the Mother Chapter once every two years.
- Tailor the bylaws of the Mother Charter to reflect the "flavor" of the local chapter.
- If desired, develop and maintain a Facebook Group for the chapter.

Simply fulfilling the responsibilities of a local agency does not, in itself, ensure a successful chapter. Proper leadership must be cultivated and the issues of growth, attrition and longevity must be addressed. These matters are discussed in another section of the SOP Book.

Example of Certificate of Acceptance

Maniacs Motorcycle Club
Local Chapter Application

Local Chapter Name: ____   Date:______________

Address: ____
      City   *State*

Point of Contact (POC) #1

Name: ____

Phone: _________________________________   Email:______________________________

Point of Contact (POC) #2

Name: ____

Phone: _________________________________   Email:______________________________

Certification

We certify the above-named chapter will strive to maintain the traditions, beliefs, and core values of the Maniacs MC. We attest the above-named chapter will meet its obligations as specified in the Mother Charter of the Maniacs Motorcycle Club.

Signatures:____   Date:______________

Pledge of Allegiance

We declare the above-named chapter will pledge allegiance to the vision and philosophy of the Maniacs MC.

Signatures:____   Date:______________

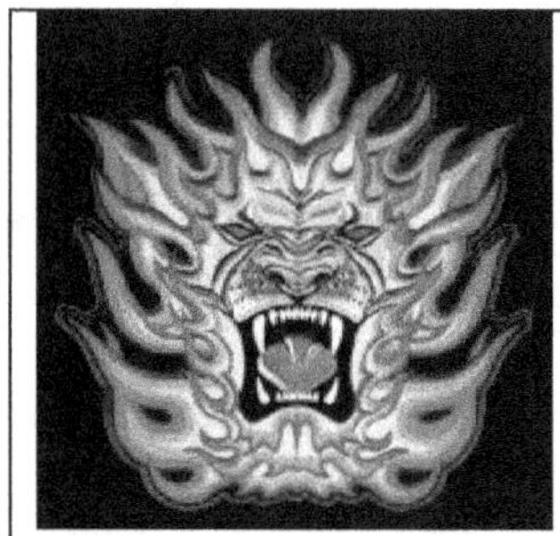

<table>
<tr><td colspan="2">Maniacs Motorcycle Club Membership Roster</td></tr>
<tr><td>Name of Local Chapter</td><td>Established Date</td></tr>
<tr><td></td><td></td></tr>
<tr><td>Years in Existence</td><td>Date Roster was last updated</td></tr>
<tr><td></td><td></td></tr>
</table>

Name	Alias
E-mail	**Phone**

Name	Alias
E-mail	**Phone**

Name	Alias
E-mail	**Phone**

Name	Alias
E-mail	**Phone**

Name	Alias
E-mail	**Phone**

Name	Alias
E-mail	**Phone**

Page _______ of _______

Official Mother Charter of the Maniacs Motorcycle Club ®™

Bylaws – Maniacs Motorcycle Club

Mission statement:
The mission of the Maniacs Motorcycle Club (MC) is to foster a spirit of camaraderie among members who share a common vision of the biker lifestyle and a common love of riding motorcycles and embracing individual freedom to its fullest.

Motto:
MFFM – Maniacs Forever and Forever Maniacs. This reflects the brotherhood bond among club members and demonstrates the high level of camaraderie, loyalty, and unconditional support among the Maniacs. All members are expected to wear a MFFM patch on the front of their club colors.

Article I – Name
This organization shall be known as the Maniacs Motorcycle Club.

Article II – Organization
In keeping with the theme of freedom, the Maniacs MC does not endorse any specific formal organizational structure. The Maniacs MC attempts to offer the more freedom to its members than ordinary motorcycle clubs. The mother charter contains very few bylaw requirements for its local chapters.

Local chapters are at liberty to tailor the bylaws of the mother charter in order to meet the unique needs and expectations of the members residing in the local chapters. The Mother Charter of the Maniacs MC recognizes the beliefs and core values of its members will change as new members are added and new local chapters are added. Having the ability to tailor the mother charter ensures the "flavor" of each local chapter remains unique in its future and truly reflects the values and beliefs of its members.

The freedom of individual chapters to add their own bylaws shall never be abused. Creation of new bylaws and formal organizational structure shall only be the result of the chapter's individual personality and the desires of its membership and never for control over its members. Our members shall never feel oppressed. The essence of our club is to simply don colors, ride our bikes, be free, and enjoy life with gusto of a biker's lifestyle.

The spirits of the original 1935 Outlaws, the original 1945 Pissed Off Bastards, the original 1946 Boozefighters, and the original 1947 Market Street Commandos never intended motorcycle clubs to have formal organizational structure with a host of bylaws and other restricted rules. In our opinion, such actions are the antithesis of a true biker lifestyle.

That said, some local chapters might grow to such a size as to necessitate formal organizational structure. Although we might tend to embrace chaos – especially since our members tend to be better equipped to deal with chaos than the average man and are usually fully capable of handling chaotic situations – there can be a point in local chapter size where formal structure is needed.

If used, formal organizational structure will usually result in the creation of an Executive Board consisting of a President, Vice-President, Secretary/Treasurer, Sergeant-at-Arms, and Road Captain.

These bylaws shall be the fundamental law of the Maniacs Motorcycle Club.

In addition to the Mother Charter, there exists the Maniacs Standard Operating Procedure (SOP) book. All members should maintain an up-to-date SOP book. Electronic copies are available for free. Hard copies can be procured through Amazon.

The Maniacs Motorcycle Club and its logo are registered trademarks.

Article III – Membership

<u>Section 1 – Full Members</u>

Full members have voting privileges. To become a full member a candidate must fill out a written application, attesting they are able to meet Maniac standards, and pledging allegiance to the vision and philosophy of the Maniacs MC, including acceptance of the traditional beliefs and core values of the local chapter.

The Membership Application form is available through the Maniacs SOP Book, the Maniacs Facebook Page, and through <u>maniacsmotorcycleclub@gmail.com</u>.

Once a candidate receives an acceptance letter, they become authorized to procure the club's colors. This consists of the Maniacs logo, a top and bottom rocker, and five patches. The placement of the club's colors must be exact.

The final step to becoming a full member is getting officially sworn-in by an active Maniac in good standing. The swearing-in ceremony varies from local chapter-to-local chapter.

Full members must possess a motorcycle. All bikes are welcome as long as they are capable of maintaining highway speeds of 65-70 mph for prolonged periods of time.

<u>Section 2 – Associate Members</u>

Associate members may not vote. To become an associate member, you must be a spouse or significant other of a full member in good standing.

Associate members may participate in club activities and events. Associate members may also wear club colors but with one important caveat – associate members are prohibited from wearing an alias patch. In place of the alias patch, the associate member must wear a generic associate member ID patch.

The associate member ID patch must be worn on the right front-side and contain the words "Associate Member." For more details on appropriate colors refer to the Maniacs SOP Book.

If associate members decide to procure and wear club colors, they are expected to maintain them according to the club's strack standards. If the associate member's status changes in their relation to the sponsoring Maniac full-member, then the associate will no longer be authorized to wear club colors unless they continue their club association through another new relationship with another full-member Maniac of the club. Otherwise, it is the previous sponsoring member's responsibility to retrieve the club's colors.

Section 3 – Prospective Members

The Maniacs Motorcycle Club does not believe in probate periods. Our founding father organizations (e.g. original 1935 Outlaws, the original 1945 Pissed Off Bastards, the original 1946 Boozefighters, and the original 1947 Market Street Commandos) did not use them and we do not use them.

Our vision of a biker lifestyle is all about freedom. Why would anyone in their right frame of mind want to oppress this feeling by requiring new applicants to go through an oppressive probate period? In our opinion, there are far better ways for new applicants to bond with the club.

Section 4 – Acceptance of Membership

Upon receipt of an acceptance letter, and possession of appropriate club colors, the applicant is required to get officially sworn-in. The swearing-in ceremony varies from local chapter-to-local chapter.

Section 5 – Duration of Membership

Maniacs MC membership is eternal.

Section 6 – Requirements for Membership in good standing

All full members are considered to be members in good standing.

A member in good standing will keep their club colors to strack standard. A member in good standing wears their club colors when riding.

A member in good standing is expected to comply with the Mother Charter bylaws and any addendum bylaws of their local chapter.

Section 7 – Resignation of Membership

MFFM is the motto. A Maniac does not resign from the Maniacs MC. However, the member does have the option to request a sabbatical from the club. Sabbaticals usually last from one year to multiple years. Sabbaticals can be used for various reasons. They can range from needing to be a caretaker for a family member, to taking a spiritual pilgrimage, to going back to school, to being temporarily incarcerated. If you are granted a sabbatical, you will be kept in the club's communication loop but are not expected to participate in club activities. Members on sabbatical leave will have their voting privileges temporarily suspended until they return to being a member in good standing.

Article IV – Code of Conduct

Ride your motorcycle as often as you can.

Put on your colors when you ride. Wear your club colors appropriately and to high standard.

Be proud of your ancestral heritage and be willing to fight to defend it.

Offer no excuses.

Family responsibilities, job responsibilities, and spiritual responsibilities always come first.

Be the best you can be and consistently seek to be better. Support other club members in their efforts to achieve the same high standards.

Demonstrate patriotism and support our nation's military.

Honor and protect the club and the communities we live in through whatever means are necessary.

Your conduct shall be consistent with the vision of Maniacs MC as spelled out in the beginning of this charter. Your conduct shall be consistent with the belief and core values of your local chapter. Although in most cases, the beliefs and core values between the mother organization and your local chapter will be aligned; in some cases, there might be an exception. In such situations, the belief and core values of your local chapter will take precedence.

Article V – Meetings/Activities
Section 1 - Meetings
Since no formal organization is required, meetings are obsolete.

Regular communications among local chapter members can be achieved through simple word-of-mouth, telephone, e-mail, maintenance of a Facebook Group Page, Skype, etc. Each chapter should decide on a preferred means of communication for its members to use.

Regular communications from the mother organization is maintained through the periodical called *Maniac Ramblings*. Local Chapters are encouraged to submit articles for publication within *Maniac Ramblings*. The goal is to publish this periodical twice per year to keep members appraised of club-wide news and events.

If the local chapter is large enough to consider formal organization with an Executive Board comprised of elected officers, and the local chapter decides to go that route, it shall hold an annual meeting. The need for other meetings is at the discretion of the local chapter. Notice of meetings shall be sent to each member through the chapter's preferred means of communication indicating meeting dates, times and places.

For the majority of local chapters (those without formal structure), club business and planned activities should be communicated through the local chapter's preferred mode of communication. Chapters without formal organization are not required to hold an annual meeting.

Section 2 – Activities
Chapter rides and activities may be suggested and organized by any club member. The vast majority of activities will simply fall under the simple act of riding motorcycles. We highly encourage regular club rides. We tend to categorize Maniac rides as advanced-notice rides or spur-of-the-moment rides. The main intent of either ride-type is to get some members together, put on your colors, and ride. That's the essence of a Maniac.

Advanced-notice rides
An advanced-notice ride is any ride/activity organized and sponsored by a chapter of the Maniacs MC. Postings for advanced-notice rides should be made through the local chapter's preferred mode of communication. If made far enough in advanced, the chapter can have the rides posted in *Maniac Ramblings* – the club's semi-annual periodical.

For most advanced-notice rides, a Road Captain should be designated. We recommend this title be rotated among your club members on a ride-by-ride basis. If the ride involves a significant number of riders, consideration should also be given into assigning Blockers. As with the Road Captains, the responsibility of Blockers should be rotated among your club members on a ride-by-ride basis.

We highly encourage local chapter participation in the charity & benefit rides of other organizations. Besides riding for a worthy cause, it gives us a great chance to dispel some of the personal prejudices and phobias others hold toward one-percenter clubs. Attempt to get favorable publicity for the Maniacs when participating in these types of rides. Local chapters are free to organize their own charity & benefit rides if desired.

Spur-of-the-moment rides

In keeping with the theme of individual freedom, spur-of-the-moment rides do not need road captains or ride rules. These are among the most common of Maniac rides. It simply involves the spontaneous action of contacting a few Maniac Brothers, donning your colors, and going out for a ride.

One of the ultimate Maniac activities – and probably the most common and enjoyable of all – is riding solo while flying your colors. Just you, the road and the wind.

The wearing of club colors is mandated on all rides. One of the few "rules" of the Maniacs MC.

Article VI – Dues/Initiation Fees

In the opinion of the Maniacs MC, a member's hard-earned money is better spent on maintaining one's motorcycle and colors than for paying unnecessary dues. We believe the act of forming and belonging to a motorcycle club should be free.

That said, some local chapters might want to maintain a permanent clubhouse. If that is the will of the majority of local chapter members, the local chapter has the option to initiate a membership fee for those purposes. However, the fee shall be capped to reflect the cost of rent, utilities and taxes in maintaining the clubhouse. If the local chapter proceeds in this direction, it will assign two members to handle collecting and dispersing monies. In addition, a General Ledger shall be kept to maintain accountable. Any full member can request a financial audit at any time if the local chapter decides to collect club dues for these purposes.

Article VII – Officers

In the opinion of the Maniacs MC, having an elected Executive Board with Officers is an unnecessary constraint that usually oppresses its membership – through the formation of unnecessary rules – rather than promoting the lifestyle of a biker [freedom from rules].

That said, some local chapters might grow to such a size as to necessitate formal organizational structure. Although we might tend to embrace chaos – especially since our members tend to be better of better stock than the average man and are usually fully capable of handling chaotic situations – there can be a point in local chapter size where formal structure is needed.

If used, formal organizational structure will usually result in the creation of an Executive Board consisting of a President, Vice-President, Secretary/Treasurer, Sergeant-at-Arms, and Road Captain.

If the local chapter decides to go this route, they will need to address the following issues:

- Officer responsibilities

- Election
- Transfer of leadership
- Terms
- Powers
- Limitations
- Vacancies

These issues should be addressed in writing and be added to the chapter's bylaws.

Creation of formal organizational structure should only be the result of the chapter's individual personality and the desires of its membership and never for control over its members. Maniacs should never feel oppressed by their local chapter. Remember the essence of the club is to simply don colors, ride bikes, be free, and enjoy life with gusto – not to create some darn enterprise.

Article VIII – Discipline

Although a Maniac is expected to have better attributes than the average person and be able to demonstrate self-disciple, there will be exceptions. On occasion, a Maniac's zeal for living life to its fullest lands them in trouble. On occasion, a Maniac's dislike for oppression lands them in trouble. On occasion, a Maniac's dislike for rules lands them trouble. Normally these exceptions only lead to mayhem – property might get damaged but no individual gets hurt in the ruckus. Shit simply happens.

However, encouraging members to let fly with the R-complex part of their brain under appropriate circumstances can result in dire consequences. It is never the intent of any Maniac to do permanent physical harm to another individual. The Maniac must realize the R-complex part of our brain sometimes blinds us to that restraining threshold. So, although a Maniac is encouraged to use his triune brain when necessary, it is equally important to have control over it.

The bottom-line is each Maniac is responsible for their own actions. Sometimes that means manning up and paying the piper. If a Maniac Brother is in trouble, do not be judgmental, be supportive. Listen to your brother's version of events and try to provide appropriate consult if requested.

A Maniac never testifies against another Maniac. We tend to handle things in-house and not air dirty laundry.

Maniacs are expected to do their own repentance. If the actions warrant it, the individual might want to self-impose a sabbatical leave from the club as part of their repentance ritual.

If the actions are egregious enough, the club chapter can vote to enforce a sabbatical on the individual. Since forced sabbaticals are a serious breech to freedom, it requires the unanimous consent of all full members within the chapter.

All Maniacs should realize the general public, including other motorcycle clubs, often have an extremely distorted perception about one-percenter motorcycle clubs. This often leads to unwarranted phobias, prejudice, and stereo-typing of those bikers who wear the 1% patch.

Maniacs can help correct those images by making self-discipline a high priority in their own lifestyle and helping other Maniac brothers make the right choices, too.

A cardinal rule for the Maniacs MC is "no permanent physical harm shall become a Maniac at the hands of another Maniac." A Maniac might be roughed up by another Maniac – usually by a fistfight – or by a group of Maniacs; but no permanent physical harm shall be done to another Maniac Brother. The Word.

Article IX – Colors
<u>Section 1 – Ownership</u>
Once procured, patches (colors) are the property of the individual member. Procurement is prohibited without first having received an acceptance letter.

<u>Section 2 – Rights</u>
The Maniacs MC's name and logo are registered trademarks. Reproduction is prohibited without expressed permission. Permission can be requested through maniacsmotorcycleclub@gmail.com.

Full-member Maniacs are considered lifetime members so this issue is moot. In regards to associate members, the original sponsoring full-member Maniac is responsible for ensuring the recovery of Maniac colors if there is any change in status regarding the associate member.

<u>Section 4 – Wearing of Colors</u>
Members are expected to wear their colors when riding their motorcycles. Wearing of colors is also expected at all club activities.

Colors shall only be worn in approved fashion (e.g. rockers, logo, and MC cube on back of leather vest/jacket; four mandated patches on front; any chapter-approved patches shall be restricted to front and shall not interfere with the placement of any mandated front patches, etc.).

Colors should be maintained to strack standards. Frequent visual inspection of the leather jacket/vest is required correct for loose and hanging threads. Click or burn the ends of these threads. Replace any stained or frayed patches as necessary.

Check the Maniacs SOP book for further details.

Article X – Chapters
Chapters are primarily based on geographical location. In population-dense areas, more than one chapter might exist. Chapters are encouraged to develop their own unique "flavor" of doing business. The flavor of each chapter should be reflective of their membership.

<u>Section 1 – Request for new Local Chapter</u>
Completed requests to establish a new Maniacs MC Chapter must be submitted in writing to through maniacsmotorcycleclub@gmail.com.

A minimum of two members is required to start a new Local Chapter.

The New Maniacs Local Chapter Application form is available through maniacsmotorcycleclub@gmail.com. It is also available through the Maniacs SOP Book and the Maniacs Facebook Page.

There are no application fees associated with starting a new chapter.

<u>**Section 2 – Mother Chapter**</u>

The location of the Mother Chapter of the Maniacs MC is kept secret to avoid infiltration by government agencies. The Mother Chapter is comprised of several key individuals who are dispersed among the local chapters.

The ONLY source of contact with the Mother Chapter is through maniacsmotorcycleclub@gmail.com.

The Mother Chapter's responsibilities:

- Maintenance of the Mother Charter.
- Approve new MMC Local Chapters.
- Issue Certificates of Acceptance to approved local chapters.
- Maintenance of the Maniac SOP Book. Local Chapters can add their own addendums to the Maniac SOP book. In particular, each local chapter should have their own list of beliefs and core values reflecting the consensus of its members. The ability to add their own addendum to the SOP book ensures each chapter develops its own unique "flavor" of doing business.
- Maintenance and publication of ***Manic Ramblings***.
- Maintenance of the Maniacs' Facebook Page.
- Approve new members. This function is normally delegated to local chapters.
- Approve membership sabbaticals. This function is normally delegated to local chapters.
- Handle third-party requests for using the club's registered trademark name and logo.

<u>**Section 3 - Local Chapters**</u>

The Local Chapter's responsibilities:

Approve new members.

Conduct swearing in ceremonies for new members.

Approve associate members.

Organize chapter rides and activities.

Ensure all members have access to the Maniac SOP Book.

Tailor the Maniac SOP book with the chapter's own addendum.

Ensure all members have access to Manic Ramblings.

Designate two members to be the main points of contact with the Mother Chapter.

Each chapter will be responsible for maintaining an updated roster of members including their contact information. This is normally the responsibility of the two members designated as being the main points of contact with the Mother Chapter.

Decide on a preferred means of communication for the chapter. Ensure chapter members are capable of communicating with one another.

Create self-improvement opportunities for its members.

If desired, develop and implement an earned-patch system.

Approve membership sabbaticals.

Tailor the by-laws of the Mother Charter to reflect the "flavor" of the local chapter.

If desired, develop and maintain a Facebook Group for the chapter.

Each Local Chapter shall survey its members belief s and core value system once every two years (more frequently if needed). The results of the survey should be shared with all chapter members and discussion should attempted as to whether to incorporate anything of significance into the chapter's by-laws.

The belief and core value survey results – and an updated membership roster with contact information – shall be forwarded to the Mother Chapter once every two years.

<u>Section 4</u> – Expulsion of a Chapter
Although chapters are encouraged to find and develop their own "flavor" of conducting business, all Maniac local chapters and members are expected to adhere to the vision and common philosophy of the Maniacs MC as pledged forth on each member's original application.

In regards to having additional chapter by-laws to the Mother Charter, they must not contradict the Mother Charter nor the intent of the Mother Charter.

In regards to having a SOP book addendum, the chapter addendum must not contradict any of the existing SOPs or their intent.

Any observed deviations in the above three areas will result in the local chapter being given an opportunity to correct the situation. Failure to correct the situation may result in expulsion of the local chapter and loss of the local chapter patch. Expulsion of any Maniac MC chapter will be communicated to all existing chapters in good standing with the Maniacs MC through ***Maniac Ramblings.***

If the local chapter is disbanded for whatever reason, members will be given the option of joining another chapter or taking sabbatical leave.

Members who continue to wear a chapter ID patch of an expulsed local chapter will suffer dire consequences.

Article XI – Amendment of Bylaws
Amendment – The Mother Charter bylaws are reassessed every two years and adjustments are made as necessary.

Proposed Amendment Process - Proposed amendments to the Mother Charter bylaws may be suggested by local chapters but not individual members. Individual members with proposals for amendments to the Mother Charter bylaws must first propose their suggested amendments to their local chapter. Once the proposal is accepted by the local chapter, it can be presented in writing to maniacsmotorcycleclub@gmail.com for consideration in the two-year reassessment.

Consideration of Amendments - Proposals for amendment to Mother Charter bylaws will be considered during each two-year reassessment process.

Submission Requirements - Proposals should be submitted in writing at least 90 days prior to the scheduled two-year reassessment process. The date for the two-year reassessment process will be published in *Maniac Ramblings*.

Maniacs MC Mother Charter Bylaws as amended 08/10/2018

Dealing with Leadership, Growth, Attrition and Longevity

The keys to a successful local chapter reside, in part, on how well you deal with leadership, growth, attrition, and longevity issues. This has nothing to do with how bad-ass an individual you might be or how bad-ass your fellow Maniac brothers might be. It all about simple people skills stuff.

Leadership and Growth

Whether the local agency has a formal organizational structure or not, leadership will eventually evolve whether formal or informal. The important point is the right type of leadership needs to evolve.

If the chapter chooses a self-serving leader, it won't go too far and its members will end up on sabbaticals and transferring to other local chapters.

Growth occurs when members are enthusiastic enough to reach out to others and bring in membership because they believe in the club's viability. People want to believe that they are a part of something greater than themselves and their contributions are meaningful. For some, simple acceptance is enough. For others having their contributions validated by recognition or acknowledgement is necessary. An effective leader knows the difference and how to capitalize on it for the good of the club.

There is no good to come from self-interested leaders whose only goal is to have some status for themselves and power over others. This usually means these people are missing something in their personal lives. In my experience, this type of leader has more ego than compassion and has few, if any, real friends. Their concern for others is usually a thin façade that quickly breaks down when challenged. Every failed local chapter usually exhibits this type of leadership.

When MC membership becomes just another obligation to be stacked against existing obligations, members will consider their other options. Most people will put family and job first and rightfully so. The "brotherhood" thing will quickly fade for a member who feels marginalized, put upon, or segregated. Being a Maniac is supposed to be something a member looks forward to amidst the daily grind much like sports, music, and the arts.

A member's spare time is limited. It is incumbent on the leadership to provide an atmosphere that makes the member glad they chose a Maniac activity will look forward to dedicating a significant portion of their personal time to the Maniacs MC. For a leader, this means being able to see it from the members' perspective.

Absolute retention of membership is virtually impossible. Yes, the Maniacs motto is "MFFD" but this is more motto is more on a spiritual and heart-felt level than on a practical level. It can be difficult to gage a person's level of dedication. The level of dedication may change due to unforeseen circumstances. Like most human social structures there will be a core of true believers who will remain steadfast. There will be a group of moderately dedicated individuals who will stay for a significant time and show a respectable level of involvement. Then there will be peripheral members who will have a low level of dedication. These outliers will be the first to go if anything controversial happens. They will enjoy wearing the patch and "being there with the group" for a while. But, when it comes to putting forth the effort to sustain the club, build a good reputation, and live up to the stated mission and goals, only a few will rise to the occasion.

A club that starts with just a few friends will not grow if the original members don't recognize that friendship should be the result of club membership not a prerequisite for it.

Members stay with the club because it fits with their lifestyle, there is little or no conflict with work, family, or other social activities. It is something they can identify with and a place where they feel accepted and comfortable. That is what future Maniac leaders need to recognize and capitalize on in order to ensure a successful local chapter.

Attrition

Internal drama is the biggest club killer. Unfortunately, MC life attracts people who love drama. The combination of excessive politics, drama, and friction among members will drive people away. This usually means someone is targeted and antagonized for the entertainment of the antagonist. Straighten out this kind of individual or get rid of them destroy your chapter. Sometimes a simple fistfight is all that is needed to straighten them out. The old-school military blanket parties can also be an effective vehicle for straightening out wayward members. Last resort is an indefinite sabbatical. But usually, most problems and internal conflicts can be solved without drama as long as steady-handed leadership is used.

Members leave because of conflict with family, work, or they find greater solace in other social activities. Too many members forget to check their egos at the door. MC life is about social interaction that results in providing some type of reward to the members. The leadership must be promoting collective harmony. A chapter that leaves its members feeling conflicted about their place will lose people until it folds.

Longevity

The real challenge in MC life is to make the chapter sustainable and solid. Long term stability depends on committed members who stay for the long haul. Longevity also requires some level of recognition and acceptance from those outside the club, like the community, and other clubs. If each member has a realistic view of their position within the chapter and feels fulfilled by that role, then longevity has a chance. Longevity only happens when leaders and members are smart enough to plan for future generations of members and leaders.

A sustainable chapter is led by people who serve the membership first, the community next, and themselves last. A practical leader knows they will be replaced eventually and should plan for it in the name of sustainability.

A sustainable chapter recognizes public perception and reputation are the only way to keep the community on your side. Consistent and ongoing efforts to build and maintain a positive public image is a challenge which must be accepted and embraced by every member. Yes, it might appear we put ourselves at a disadvantage by choosing to wear the 1% patch and reaping all the unwarranted discrimination attached to it. But that's our choice. A biker's lifestyle is all about freedom, and we will be damned before we fall under the auspices of some oppressive organization like the American Motorcycle Association trying to tell us what we can and cannot do as a motorcycle club.

Biker Culture – Why choose the 1% Patch

I mentioned in the Preface section of this book it had a two-fold purpose. I am repeating one of the intentions in the back part of the SOP book because most folks do not read Prefaces, and more importantly, it really deserves reinforcement.

One purpose of the SOP book is to destroy the myth of one-percenter motorcycle clubs as criminal elements.

Some readers might be disappointed with this book. Maybe there were originally expecting to discover the top secret, inner workings of a nihilistic gang of rapists and pillagers who run roughshod over anyone in their path. Get real, man.

One-percenters are not the Sons of Anarchy or the Mayans MC. It is not the distorted presentations of motorcycle clubs shown in Gangland. That's pure Hollywood hype. Stuff to make you turn on the channel and watch the program. The real life of a biker who wears a 1% patch would probably bore you to death. It is basically the simple act of riding a motorcycle and enjoying the feeling of freedom it brings.

One-percenters are not the Jack Reacher-gone-bad type of biker either. That is the biker who is constantly kicking ass [and always winning every fight even against unsurmountable odds] and bedding every hot-looking chick crossing their path (yep, even female pediatric surgeons – get real Tara). This type of one-percenter is what's commonly portrayed in popular fiction books (why else read it?); and unfortunately, this image is also commonly portrayed (to varying degrees) in supposed auto-biographies of one-percent bikers. They are laughing all the way to the bank. These are usually washed-out individuals who are only legends in their own mind. Pure entertainment – with a smidgen of truth at best – but that is what sells books.

The truth is most one-percenters are your average boring person. We simply like to ride motorcycles and embrace what we term the biker lifestyle. We are identical to ninety-nine percenters – although some prejudiced, narrow-minded, imbeciles might hold a different view. Both groups like to ride motorcycles in a group. The only difference is ninety-nine percenters allow themselves to become subservient to the American Motorcycle Association. One-percenters are subservient to no one. Since ninety-nine percenters do not mind being under the auspices of the ANA, you might find their biker lifestyles a little too constrained for your taste. Indeed, most 99% MC fail because of that flaw – "too many rules."

In contrast, one-percenters answer to no one. We epitomize the biker's lifestyle and the freedom it expresses. That might make 1% clubs a tad more rebellious; but heck, what do you expect from a group that has a serious distain for "needing" to follow rules.

In reality, there is little difference among the various motorcycle clubs. We fully welcome 99% clubs to Maniac parties and to join in on Maniac activities. That is if your club allows you to associate with us. If your club prohibits such association, do yourself a favor and tell them to kiss your ass and jump over to the Maniac brotherhood. Get a taste of the true biker's lifestyle and you will gladly wear the 1% patch with pride.

The other interesting thing is many 99% clubs are really 1% clubs but do not know it or simply are afraid to acknowledge it.

Many 99% clubs do not pay AMA dues. Many 99% clubs do not adhere to AMA standards. Guess what? By definition, you are really a 1% club. If your club falls under this category, put on a 1% patch and wear it with pride. Join forces with the Maniacs, and other 1% clubs, in helping us overcome the prejudices and stereotypes we face. Let your rebellious nature come out.

Also, many 99% clubs know they are 1% clubs by both definition and in heart (fuck you AMA). They are simply afraid to acknowledge it. They have bought into myths that if they wear a 1% patch then any neighboring 1% clubs will kick their ass. Fictitious bullshit and urban legend. If your club falls under this category come join us at the next Maniac party or activity. See for yourself what's real. After seeing the real deal, do your club a favor and put on the 1% patch. Let your rebellious nature come out and be proud to show it.

Related to the 99% clubs listed above, there are also many 99% clubs who know they are 1% clubs by both definition and in heart and would readily acknowledge it – no fear of violence here – but simply do not want to put up with the general hazzle and prejudice of law enforcement and the general public. Most of all, it is you guys that need to come out of the closet. You know the real deal. Put on the 1% patch and stand with us. Let your rebellious nature come out and be proud to show it.

Why are real 1% clubs feeling the need to operate under the guise of a 99% club? Out-of-control government and out-of-control media are the culprits. At one time, the media went to great lengths to maintain their integrity in reporting accurate facts. Those days are long gone. Now, if it is not sensationalized, it is not reported. It does not take much imagination to visualize the damage this has caused to the reputations of 1% clubs. Yep, we are all a nihilistic gang of rapists and pillagers who run roughshod over anyone in their path.

Government has not been helpful, either. Governments tend to be really frightened by autonomous groups who embrace freedom. Anarchy scares the bejesus out of them. But most 1% are not anti-government. Indeed, almost all 1% clubs are extremely patriotic and fully respect our military. It is the size of the government where there is an issue – especially when it attacks our freedoms.

Here is a dirty secret about big federal government. As the size increases, and the money pie (federal budget) remains the same, the agencies need to start justifying their degree of importance in order to pocket their fair share of the money pie. Sounds like a reasonable mechanism if you assume each agency has integrity and will report accurate facts. But the truth of the matter is the agencies in federal government have gone in the same direction as our media. Sensationalize it. Those who sensationalize get more of the money pie. Let's face it, we live in an age of sensationalism. Unfortunately, government sensationalism has resulted in 1% clubs being labeled a nihilistic gang of rapists and pillagers who run roughshod over anyone in their path.

The truth of the matter is those who wear the 1% patch embrace a culture based on the concepts of freedom, loyalty, honor, respect and a love for riding motorcycles. By their nature, one-percenters also tend to be a bit rebellious due to their dislike for oppressive rules and other attacks on their coveted freedoms.

The truth of the matter is those who wear the 1% patch have a passion for a free society where you are judged by your actions, not your appearance. The desire to be left alone and not be harassed. This includes the self-respect to be able to stand your ground and not allow anyone to abuse or disrespect your person. Maybe, mainstream society is more tolerant of abuse/disrespect from others; but no one cares more about the concepts of freedom and honor than a one-percent biker.

One-percenters protect the elderly, young and the weak from being abused. One-percenters will not physically harm you unless you are caught preying on one of the classes of people just mentioned. That does not mean it's OK to shoot your mouth off at a one-percenter. That's likely to earn you a smack upside your head.

One-percenter motorcycle clubs are no more criminals than other historical groups fighting government discrimination, policies of oppression, and attacks on their freedoms. Patriots were considered outlaws. Many civil rights groups in the past were considered outlaws. Many current civil rights groups are considered outlaws. Peacefully demonstrating environmentalists are considered outlaws. For crying out loud, ancient governments described Jesus as an outlaw.

We will not hide from our true heritage. We wear the 1% patch with pride.

Brotherhood

The degree of brotherhood varies from local chapter to local chapter and from individual Maniac to individual Maniac. That is why we worded one of the Maniac objectives as "To offer a brotherhood ↔ family ↔ friendship bond with other Maniac members."

At one end of the spectrum, you have individual Maniacs who might place little value on brotherhood. They did not join to specifically find friends. Maybe, they joined simply to be able to ride in groups. Group riding tends to be safer simply because of being more visible in traffic. Maybe, they joined to get more pussy. The bad boy image does tend to get more than its fair share of chicks.

At the other end of the spectrum, you have individual Maniacs who place immense value on brotherhood. They joined specifically to have an extended family.

Regardless of an individual's perspective on brotherhood, the Maniacs MC believes brotherhood is an important element in the life of all Maniacs.

From an academic standpoint, a brotherhood forms over an expanded time frame where shared experiences evolve into mutually held beliefs by people who are engaged in similar activities in a like-minded way. A kinship bond forms among those involved that tends to be greater than other social or family bonds.

In other words, a brotherhood forms when a club member's bond with his fellow members is stronger than the bond they have others outside the club. But that is pure academia crap. There may be some Maniacs who have stronger ties to fellow club members than their own families, but that is not the norm – nor is it expected from the average Maniac.

That is why we worded the Maniac MC objective as "To offer a brotherhood ↔ family ↔ friendship bond with other Maniac members." We expect most members to put family, job, and God first in their list of priorities and rightfully so. If the individual Maniac forms brotherhood bonds with other members that transcends this expectation to where the Maniac brothers become extended family that is great. That is always something worth striving for.

As a Maniac, you are expected to continually improve your mind, body and soul through personal self-motivation – to better yourself. You should also be supportive and encourage other Maniac brothers in doing the same thing.

Ride Hard Party Hard

The phrase "Ride Hard Party Hard" is mentioned in the club's description, in the objectives of the maniacs MC, and under the Maniacs MC's core values. What is meant by ride hard party hard?

You might have noticed in two of the three places it was mentioned with celebrating life and living life to its fullest. Indeed, they are certainly related to one another.

The term is also reflective of the definition of Maniac. The definition of a Maniac entails a person characterized by an inordinate or ungovernable enthusiasm for something. With that kind of moniker as your name, how would you party?

Let's take another definition of Maniac. The definition of a Maniac is a person who behaves in a very wild way. Dahh! How would you live up to your namesake?

On a serious note, it simply reflects how we approach life in general – with full colors and gusto!

Riding Hard

Safety is first. If you have new members who are relatively new to riding motorcycles, encourage them to take a certified safety course. Alternatively, consider having your local agency do their own safety course.

Another consideration beyond group rides and partying is having regular motorcycle skills practice sessions in some big public parking lot. Practice things like emergency braking (use those four paws), circles/figure 8's, sharp right turns from a start, slow speed riding, swerving practice, slalom games for steering, etc.

So, what does riding-hard mean? Again, I simply refer you back to the definition of a Maniac – enough said!

No, riding-hard does not mean riding with a boner, but that does relate nicely to our next subject.

Partying Hard

This is really a façade. Our sole intent here is simply to get nice-looking ladies to lose their inhibitions and take advantage of them. Geez, my one-percenter honesty is showing forth way too much. Of course, we would not force ourselves, nor would we take advantage of them. Obviously, hot unbridled sex is a fantastic outcome of partying hard; but the desire would have to be mutual.

If you want the real meaning of partying hard, I refer you back to the definition of a Maniac. It does not get much clearer.

Some folks might think this is a contradiction in terms since the Maniacs MC places a high value on health, staying in shape and diet; but it is not like we are party animals. Maniacs do not party everyday of the week. It's simple when we do – it tends to be with inordinate or ungovernable enthusiasm.

Local agencies are responsible for setting their own guidelines on what's acceptable and what is forbidden at Maniac-sponsored parties. The Mother Chapter finds most forms of alcohol and recreational drugs are acceptable. The Mother Chapter also finds the use most psychoactive plants and mushrooms are acceptable as forms of spiritual enlightenment. The use of heroin, meth, and designer drugs are highly discouraged.

Heroin might produce blissful states but is extremely difficult to control.

Meth is the drug of choice for many biker's, and I can understand why; but it has the tendency to unleash the R-complex part of our triune brain. Being violent has its place, but not when it is artificially induced. Add on meth's predisposition to induce paranoia and you end up with a walking keg of dynamite. Totally convinced, this is what resulted in the Waco shootout. If you have meth heads in your local chapter get them help – even if it involves fists or a blanket party to get them to listen and seek help.

Designer drugs can be totally benign and produce blissful states but the problem lies in the unknown. You really do not know what you are getting when you experiment with designer drugs. There are many recreational drugs out there that produce very nice experiences where you know with reliability what the side-effects might be – stick with a known if you use recreational drugs.

Reputation

With the damage done by Hollywood, writers whose sole interest is in selling books no matter the degree of embellishment, and the government, one would think we do not give a fuck about what others think of us.

I hope by reading this book, you feel otherwise. If you were an individual without prejudice to one-percenter clubs from the start, then bless your soul, and please ensure you pass on your genetic material. The world needs more folks like you.

Of course, we care about the Maniacs' reputation. We just have more of a battle on our hands because we have chosen to wear the 1% patch.

A significant portion of this book is about club colors. As should be apparent, the correct wearing and maintenance of them is a high Maniac priority. How your club colors are worn and look often makes the first impression of the club on others. First impressions are critically important – it's simple human nature.

The reputation of your chapter among outsiders is just as important as the internal morale within your chapter. Let's face it, people talk. If your chapter is a dramatic revolving door for members, it won't be long before this is what you are known for. Eventually, no-one will want to join your chapter if it is known for ejecting or driving away members.

The reputation of your chapter among neighboring clubs is also important. Do not try to "steal" members from other chapters or other motorcycle clubs. Rest on the laurels of own your chapter. Invite the neighboring clubs to some of your parties and rides. Get to know them and try to cultivate an atmosphere of respect. We all share a common bond – riding motorcycles – build on it. Of course, you will probably have more in common with other one-percenter clubs; but do not neglect reaching out to ninety-nine percenter clubs. Remember, many of them are really one-percenters by definition and in heart but simply do not wear the 1% patch for reasons previously discussed in this book.

Public Image

Public image and reputation go hand-in-hand. Yes, we have a significant uphill battle with both. However, Maniacs are not quitters. We will not discard our 1% patches and hide among the other motorcycle clubs. We shall overcome. Chapter-by-chapter. Community-by-community. We will persevere. Remember the tribal lion's head on our logo – we are divinely chosen.

Again, it all starts with how you wear and maintain your Maniac colors. Do not let this standard slip. Be strack! If your colors are not up to snuff, do not wear them until you get them back up to standard.

Your local chapter and members should look for opportunities to form alliances with other community clubs and organizations to be able to do some good for others. Use the local press to your advantage to shed some light on the good things you do for the local community.

Ensure your members vote and encourage other community citizens to vote. If they can assist others getting to polling places, it will even be better. If we don't vote, and encourage others to vote, we will never stop the Washington Whale. Check out the Libertarian Party. Our club values appear most closely aligned with Libertarian Party's platform. The Democratic and Republican parties are both lost causes. They are too entrenched and have too many vested interests to really decrease the size of the federal government. Simply expect more government, subsequently more laws and rules, and consequently more attacks on your freedoms.

Holy shit! The blacks were emancipated in 1863. At the rate the Democrats and Republicans are going, we will need another Emancipation Act before the 2063. By then, the government will have enslaved all poor folk. Not with balls and chains, but with a dependency on entitlement programs zapping all sense of self-worth and incentive to do better. By then, the government will have enslaved all middle-class folk. Not in the form of balls and chains, but with excessive taxes to fund the bloated Washington Whale. Discretionary spending for middle-class will be like the lower classes incentive to work – zilch! There will be so many damn federal laws, rules and regulations, folks will not only feel like they are enslaved, they will feel like they are incarcerated. By 2063, 98% of America will be enslaved by an oppressive government that thinks it is doing good for its citizens but is too dumb to realize it is enslaving them just the same as if they put balls and chains on us.

Yes, big government threatens your freedom.

Pardon the rambling, my 1% nature is coming out. Back to reputations.

It is important for all local chapters to take initiative and make the Maniacs MC become an asset to their community. Do not wait for them to come to you. Take the initiative and go to them and ask how you and the local chapter can help. They might be taken aback – after all aren't we supposed to be a nihilistic gang of rapists and pillagers who run roughshod over anyone in their path.

What it boils down to is this reality – if want the public's respect, you must earn it. Since we wear the 1% patch, this becomes harder because we must overcome lots of bias and prejudice. But in the long run, we shall overcome.

Relationships with other MC and Law Enforcement

You have already reviewed snippets of information on the subject of relationships with other motorcycle clubs but I have not broached the important subject of relationships with law enforcement.

Relationships with other motorcycle clubs

As mentioned, we believe in being supportive of all motorcycle clubs. Although our value system is more aligned with our fellow one-percenter brothers, we still treat ninety-nine percenters as our brothers, too. The real deal is most motorcycle clubs get along fine with each other. It is Hollywood, big government, and the media who exaggerate and sensationalize isolated incidents. These culprits love to antagonize infighting among motorcycle clubs. Unfortunately, some clubs – both one-percenters and ninety-nine percenters – have bought into this bogus dissention trap. In the eyes of a Maniac, if you ride a motorcycle you are treated as brother. Let's stop being dumb stooges and bury our hatchets. We all face enough prejudice without being prejudicial to each other.

As a sidebar – it would not surprise me the least if the government planted undercover agents within one-percenter clubs for the sole purpose of trying to antagonizing infighting among motorcycle clubs. Keep a close eye on any new members who always seems to be having a "beef" with other clubs.

As discussed, the reputation of your chapter among neighboring clubs is also important. Do not try to "steal" members from other chapters or other motorcycle clubs. Rest on the laurels of own your chapter. Invite the neighboring clubs to some of your parties and rides. Get to know them and try to cultivate an atmosphere of respect. We all share a common bond – riding motorcycles – build on it. Of course, you will probably have more in common with other one-percenter clubs; but do not neglect reaching out to ninety-nine percenter clubs. Remember, many of them are really one-percenters in their soul but simply do not wear the 1% patch for reasons previously discussed in this book.

Relationships with Law Enforcement

It is extremely unfortunate law enforcement labels all bikers who wear the 1% patch as outlaws or criminals.

You might be really surprised how many front-line law enforcement staff feel differently. Since they are in the trenches, they know the real deal. It is the upper echelon of law enforcement that's the problem. These upper echelon jackasses have lost touch with their troops. They are the ones who prostitute themselves before budget committees and are the ones profiling us as outlaws and criminals. Part of it is that old "got to create dangers that scare the public in order to justify getting a bigger piece of the money pie." The other part is pure prejudice and bias. The upper echelon of law enforcement is not immune to the sensationalism brought on by Hollywood and the media. Yep, upper echelon law enforcement are the ones who decided to classify bikers who wear the 1% patch as outlaws or criminals. Shit, the majority of them have no ideal how the term one-percenter was derived. That makes the reader of this SOP book more educated than most upper-echelon law enforcement.

Totally different story with front-line law enforcement – the ones in the trenches – the ones who know the real deal about bikers who wear the 1% patch.

We have much in common with our front-line brothers in blue. Yeah, you might get one who gets on a power trip and tries to intimidate you. Especially, if you are by yourself and there is a big size difference. Yeah, there are rookies, too, who haven't been in the trenches long enough to know better and whose higher ups have warned them we are all a nihilistic gang of rapists and pillagers who run roughshod over anyone in their path. Yep, usually the new rookie has also been biased by the sensationalism brought on by Hollywood and the media. Those individuals might be rough to deal with; but in general, you will find most front-line law enforcement very supportive of our lifestyle.

Besides those exceptions, we do have many things in common. We both tend to be patriotic and are extremely supportive of our military. We both tend to hold the concepts of loyalty, honor, and respect in high regards.

We both want to protect the elderly, young and the weak from being abused. We both want to protect are communities and make them better places to live in.

Indeed, how did we ever allow society to set us against each other?

I highly encourage your local chapter to reach out to the community's front-line law enforcement staff. Yeah, there might be some bad apples but usually your efforts will rewarded ten-fold. Less hazzling of club members, less checkpoints, less tickets, less confrontation. It really is a win-win situation.

You can always reciprocate any goodwill received by any inquiring whether there are any community punks who might need an attitude adjustment. We can be very good at handling those problems since we do not have to operate under the same constraints. Alliances can help both parties make the community a better place to live in.

Unfortunately, upper-echelon law enforcement is not reachable and I would not waste time with them. Their sensationalized opinion of us is too engrained. Their job is to maintain status quo and enforce the policies of government. The biker lifestyle will always be a threat to them because it is based on freedom.

But by all means, reach out to your front-line law enforcement. It goes hand-in-hand with reaching out to the community and building a reputation and public image. Simple reach-out and follow Maniac SOP.

You might even start to see some of the other motorcycle clubs who are not AMA associated put on the 1% patch. Now, that would be real progress.

Pissed Off

I mentioned the Maniacs MC is patriotic and supports our nation's military. You will find this true in most motorcycle clubs. It is something that bonds us together – both 99%-ers and 1%-ers. All of us tend to hold the flag in utmost reverence as the vast majority of us are veterans.

Reverence for the flag is ingrained in every schoolchild who has quailed at the thought of letting it touch the ground, in every citizen moved by pictures of it being raised at Iwo Jima or planted on the moon, in every veteran who has ever heard taps played at the end of a Memorial Day parade, in every gold-star mother who treasures a neatly folded emblem of her family's supreme sacrifice.

Yet, shortly before the Fourth of July in 1989—two centuries after the Constitution of the United States took effect—five nincompoops on the Supreme Court declared that the government could not stop citizens from desecrating the nation's flag.

The twisted logic behind their decision was the flag's high reverence was precisely why federal and state laws to protect the flag were in violation of free-speech protections. The flag is highly revered because it represents the land of the free, and that freedom includes the ability to use or abuse the flag in protest.

Unfortunately, too many good folks accepted that moronic decision with a fight. Today, you still many high officials and responsible individuals simply accepting it as the right decision.

I beg to differ! Here are several reasons why this twisted-logic decision should be reversed.

Four Supreme Court Justices did not agree. It was a 5-4 decision. There is no reason to assume the majority had it right. Indeed, quite the opposite.

Here are the five Supreme Court Justices who decided our revered flag could be desecrated:

- William Brennan
- Thurgood Marshall
- Harry Blackmum
- Antonio Scalia
- Anthony Kennedy

Guess, how many of the above ever fought in a war zone for our nation's flag and witnessed a brother-in-arms making the ultimate sacrifice?

You betcha, not one of them!

In fairness, William Brennan did do legal work in an Ordnance Division in WWII but he entered as a pampered Major and was never in harm's way. Anthony Kennedy was in the National Guard for one year – but that raises its own questions. How did, he get away with doing one-year in the National Guard while the war in Vietnam was raging on?

Neither Thurgood Marshall, nor Harry Blackmum, nor Antonio Scalia ever served in our nation's military.

Are you getting the picture? It's tantamount to a black person being convicted by an all-white jury.

These five guys basically slapped every veteran and their family members in the face. From the brave few who raised the flag at Iwo Jima to all the gold-star mothers who treasure the neatly folded emblem of their family's supreme sacrifice hanging on the mantel piece.

Prior to the decision, 48 of the 50 states had laws prohibiting the desecration of the American flags. There were also several federal laws doing the same thing. The decision of the five guys without any meaningful military experience – where honoring the flag is of paramount important and something many would be willing to make the ultimate sacrifice for – reversed it all. They basically said 48 different states had it all wrong and several federal laws had it all wrong – you can't protect our flag. Not to mention that the other four Supreme Court Justices had it all wrong.

And these five guys have the audacity to be buried at Arlington Cemetery. Too bad George Patton is buried at Luxembourg. If he was buried at Arlington, he would be kicking ass on five Supreme Court Justices.

Justice William Rehnquist was spot on when he wrote in his dissent:

"The American flag, then, throughout more than 200 years of our history, has come to be the visible symbol embodying our Nation. It does not represent the views of any particular political party, and it does not represent any particular political philosophy. The flag is not simply another "idea" or "point of view" competing for recognition in the marketplace of ideas. Millions and millions of Americans regard it with an almost mystical reverence regardless of what sort of social, political, or philosophical beliefs they may have. I cannot agree that the First Amendment invalidates the Act of Congress, and the laws of 48 of the 50 States, which make criminal the public burning of the flag."

What to take a guess about Rehnquist's military service? Yep, served four years from 1943-1946.

Needless to say , I am pissed about today's high officials, and other supposed responsible individuals, who simply accept this matter as if it were a unanimous decision. As if it were irrefutably the right decision.

Maybe, if the NFL players really understood the controversial legality of this decision, they would have behaved differently in the playing of the national anthem. I know you did not intend to offend veterans and many other Americans with your protests. But it does not matter what you intended, your actions did offend us. If you ever served in our military you would understand this matter. Five Supreme Court Justices never really did and got it all wrong.

Personally, I would love for several of you to party with the Maniacs MC. It would be a good time. I am sure you would especially enjoy the blanket party at the end.

I am sharing this "Pissed Off" section to let others know. The law might allow you to desecrate the flag but Maniacs do not allow it. Want to see the Complex-R brain in action? Try testing us.

Maniacs Motorcycle Club
Membership Application

Full Name: ____ Date:_______________

Last   First   M.I.

Address: ____

Street Address   Apartment/Unit #

____

City   State   ZIP Code

Phone: _______________________________ Email:_______________________________

Local Chapter's Name (if known): ____

Preferred Alias (if desired): ____

I have reviewed the background history of the Maniacs MC. I have reviewed the objectives, beliefs, and core values of the Maniacs MC.

I personally attest to being able to meet Maniac standards.

Signature: _______________________________________ Date:_______________________

I have reviewed the vision statement and philosophy of the Maniacs MC. I personally pledge allegiance to the vision and philosophy of the Maniacs MC.

Signature: _______________________________________ Date:_______________________

Maniacs Motorcycle Club
Local Chapter Application

Local Chapter Name: ____ Date:______________

Address: ____
         City   *State*

Point of Contact (POC) #1

Name: ____

Phone: _____________________________________ Email:_________________________________

Point of Contact (POC) #2

Name: ____

Phone: _____________________________________ Email:_________________________________

We certify the above-named chapter will strive to maintain the traditions, beliefs, and core values of the Maniacs MC. We attest the above-named chapter will meet its obligations as specified in the Mother Charter of the Maniacs Motorcycle Club.

Signatures:____ Date:__________________

We declare the above-named chapter will pledge allegiance to the vision and philosophy of the Maniacs MC.

Signatures:____ Date:__________________

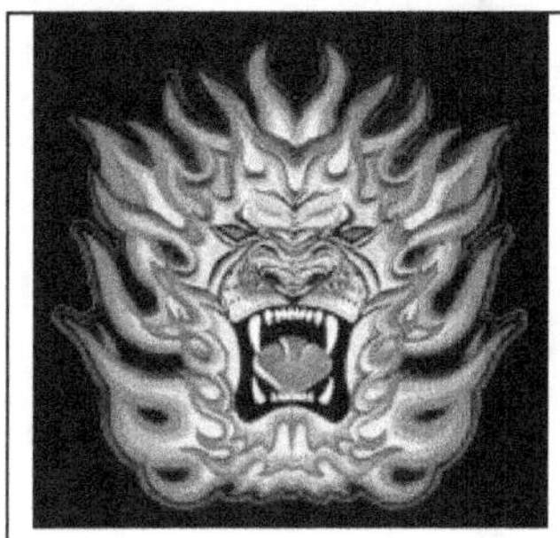

Maniacs Motorcycle Club Membership Roster

Name of Local Chapter	Established Date
Years in Existence	Date Roster was last updated

Name		Alias
E-mail		Phone

Name		Alias
E-mail		Phone

Name		Alias
E-mail		Phone

Name		Alias
E-mail		Phone

Name		Alias
E-mail		Phone

Name		Alias
E-mail		Phone

Page _______ of _______

www.ingramcontent.com/pod-product-compliance
Lightning Source LLC
Chambersburg PA
CBHW080036260726
48658CB00007B/2626